THE FURNITURE OF GERRIT THOMAS RIETVELD

DANIELE BARONI

THE FURNITURE OF GERRIT THOMAS RIETVELD

BARRON'S, Woodbury, New York

Special thanks are due to Elizabeth Eskes-Rietveld for kindly making available some of her father's unpublished drawings and sketches.
We must also thank: Wil Berteux of the Stedelijk Museum, Amsterdam, for granting permission for some important biographical documents to be published; Filippo Alison, for his suggestions concerning the arrangement of the text and his help in the task of reconstructing some prototypes; Henny van den Berg, for checking the Dutch terms and translating some passages.

First U.S. Edition 1978 by Barron's Educational Series, Inc.

© Copyright 1977 by Gruppo Editoriale Electa S.p.A.
Printed in Italy.

All inquiries should be addressed to:
Barron's Educational Series, Inc.
113 Crossways Park Drive
Woodbury, New York 11797

Library of Congress Catalog Card No.77-17883

International Standard Book No. 0-8120-5201-3

Library of Congress Cataloging in Publication Data
Baroni, Daniele.
    The Furniture of Gerrit Thomas Rietveld.
    Translation of I mobili di Gerrit Thomas Rietveld.
    Bibliography: p.
    1. Rietveld, Gerrit Thomas, 1888-1964.
    2. Furniture
—Netherlands—History—20th century. I. Title.
NK2570.R43B3713 1977   749.2'9492   77-17883
ISBNO-8120-5201-3

PRINTED IN ITALY

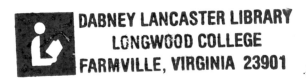

Table of Contents

The bourgeois ideals which nurtured the growth of nationalism and shattered the Europe of the decade 1910–20 brought into being at the same time, through their intrinsic contradiction, the conditions whereby artistic expression could respond to the new ethical values of the incipient industrial civilization. For the artists of the avant-garde *who sought a new kind of relationship with society, impressionism and art nouveau appeared as movements crystallizing their emphasis on aesthetic values. The urge for renewal obviously first showed itself in that part of Europe which did not suffer the burden of war—the Netherlands—and it was here that the first signs of a new attitude became manifest. Of the theoretical and cultural approach developed by the principal leaders of the movement and transferred to the practical sphere of operation at the same time, the way of viewing the artist's situation in society as a whole was of paramount importance throughout the duration of the period and determined the actual form taken by their production. The figure of the artist as a member of society, identifiable with the "common consciousness of the time," was referred to forcefully and repeatedly—very frequently in didactic rather than merely explanatory terms—by Mondrian and by Van Doesburg especially, in the course of lectures and the pages of* De Stijl. *This journal which first appeared in 1917 represented the manifesto of the movement. Its contributors were intelligent people who were very active in the panorama of the plastic and figurative arts of the period. From this time onward the supporters of De Stijl pursued their objective, which had already been precisely formulated and delineated in their aversion to naturalism: to arrive at an objective art which would be essential in its concreteness. Called Nieuwe Beelding, or neoplasticism, this art would be attained by rejecting all the subjective content of the creative process so that, for example, the constituent elements of a chair could be simple wooden listels used as if produced by machinery, without any cuts or grooves made in them. The aim of purifying the means of expression in order to arrive at an objective aesthetic result seemed to reveal a new ethics which, by transcending mere artistic creation, would come to pervade all other human activities until it attained a* universal character *which was understood as the "equilibrium of equivalent relationships." Daily life would then acquire a new style, controlled in a special way by the order of things (not humans!). The De Stijl movement, which had arisen from the minds of a few individuals, would come to represent the collective dimension of all social production. It was a process more fascinating as an idea than likely to be realized and has led more than one historian to consider De Stijl the prelude to an authentic democratic form of society made up of people imbued with Marxist ideology. The question of whether or not De Stijl favored socialism is of little importance if one remains exclusively in view of the results of their operation, which without doubt contained a high proportion of theory. But the relevance of this question becomes considerable when one realizes that an understanding of it and its side effects are necessary in order to clarify the artistic tendencies and ideologies of our time. In my view, and evaluating them also against the background of the Platonic ideal of beauty and the writings of Kandinsky by which they were inspired, the aesthetic doctrines of neoplasticism seemed to correspond to theoretical principles of genuine syncretistic idealism, precisely at the points where they tended to encompass the universal law and spirit of art and to determine the common denominator among artists through their need for abstraction, simplification, or, in other words, a perception of reality without error and fantasy. The development of the ideas of the De Stijl movement followed a course which was not really chronological and coherent; during the years of its existence various mutations, sometimes downright contradictory ones, took place within the movement. The center from which these ideas radiated was Rotterdam where painters and architects, among them Oud, Berlage, and Van Doesburg, exchanged ideas about cubism, futurism, etc. Other artists who were working in the same years in Amsterdam were influenced by quite different sources, especially Dutch art nouveau, and they created the aesthetic movement known and represented by the journal* Wendingen, *of which De Klerk was the best representative. There is no doubt that when neoplasticism later took concrete form it owed much to the cultural stimulus and discussion which radiated from these two centers, which though so different set for themselves a common objective.*

The first example of the new mode of expression came from Oud who was not ignorant of the more tawdry aspects of organic architecture introduced into Holland by Robert van't Hoff, who had been directly associated with Frank Lloyd Wright in America. There were some plans for holiday homes which were never built, and in the same year (1917) the construction of the Allegonda villa and the De Vonk building, which clearly bore the marks of the "destruction of baroque painting, of morphoplasticism, of the curve, precisely because none of these was capable of expressing the new spirit of the time and incarnating the idea of a new spiritual and human culture. . . ." The term baroque *was used to signify everything which did not aspire to the ultimate essence, whereas spatial figurativism—the formal reflection of the new culture—was devoted to the straight line, to rectangles of fundamental values, in a mutual rhythmical relationship against a white background. In other words, the effect was just like the paintings produced in the same year by Mondrian, Van Doesburg, and Van der Leck.*

The same degree of attention was shown in design. Van Doesburg himself designed interiors for Oud, considering them to be integrating elements of a unitary architectural composition and thereby introducing a new practice corresponding to contrapuntal composition, or a new style in the logical and independent collaboration between the two confluent arts, painting and architecture. Even the apparent complexity of the title suggested by Berlage for the first number of the journal was reduced to a pure geometrical synthesis. The logotype was made by Vilmos Huszar, a painter who had been a member of the group from the time it was first set up.

Rietveld joined the artistic circle in 1919, the year when Van Doesburg was most active in forming relationships with French, Italian, German, Belgian, and Russian artists and introducing them to the program of neoplasticism. Rietveld's contribution to the movement was very soon of substantial importance, and his specific field was in the design and construction of furniture rather than in architecture. His first objects—an armchair, a cupboard, and a seat—corresponded with the aesthetic principles of the group. But where his absorption of these principles was even more apparent was in the house he designed in 1923 and built in Utrecht in the following year. Because of its clarity of intention and structure, this house represents even today the typical example of the new concept of building, which was given the name De Stijl by the group and interpreted in a highly stable and orthodox manner.

The objects which were produced during this period, especially armchairs and upright seats, are rightly famous throughout the world more than ever today. They bear the visible signs of the purification of natural form which placed emphasis on the spirit of the work, no longer considered from an emotional point of view, but for its material quality. Rietveld's method of composition was perfectly in line with the analytical method advocated by the group, which from then on was reflected clearly in all his works. The house in Utrecht may be said to exemplify the ideas which Mondrian expressed in his Essays: *"When I observe the sea, sky, or stars, it occurs to me that their plastic function should be indicated by means of a multiplicity of vertical and horizontal criss-cross lines. . . . In order to create pure reality by plastic means, it is necessary to reduce natural forces [form and color, etc.] to constant formal elements, and natural colors to the basic colors. The aim is not to create other forms and special colors, with all their limitations, but to strive to embellish them in the interests of a more complete unity."*

We are left with one more question which must be considered, at the same time realizing that certain other aspects of the movement which are of equal importance have not yet been mentioned, such as its relationship with machinery, its connections with contemporary artistic movements in other countries, and Rietveld's collaboration with the Bauhaus. These matters are adequately and exhaustively discussed in the course of the text. Also, one must not overlook the fact that while Rietveld did not fulfill a primary theoretical role and in fact did not join the group until it had enjoyed more than a year of activity, he immediately became one of its most outstanding members, and when this period is viewed from today, he is seen as a pioneer of the movement whose ideas took concrete shape precisely through his own works. It seems, in fact, that his apprenticeship to a cabinetmaker (as a boy of eleven), his work as a jewelry designer, and his later contact with Klaarhamer, provided Rietveld with the manual skills which enabled him to understand and grasp the concrete reality of objects, out of which the development of any kind of artistic discourse must flow.

Rietveld's designs for interiors still arouse the same amazement and admiration today that Van Doesburg felt when he described them as "true abstract sculptures of the interiors of the future." He was speaking of the articles produced in 1919—the armchair and upright seat—which evoke the impression of masterpieces never to be surpassed. While it is true that they owe their existence to their everyday function, they represent at the same time the substantiation of the principle formulated by all the promoters of De Stijl together. The famous "Red and Blue" already expressed the criteria of elementary "antistatic" countercomposition formulated later by Van Doesburg with the introduction of the oblique line, and accepted very reluctantly by Mondrian. The sloping planes of the armchair oppose a static architectonic structure to the force of gravity, introducing into the total geometrical space the dissonant and conclusive elements of horizontal and vertical tensions. Finally, apart from its adherence to the aims of understanding and knowledge established by the previous publications in this same series, a further justification for the present study lies in its nonacademic interpretation of the situation of Rietveld in the events and ideas which make up the visual arts, architecture, and design in the first half of this century. Of course, biographers have concentrated on the social problems and cultural climate which inspired Rietveld, and today we have at our disposal a complete "profile of the artist." But when one undertakes a study of his work one is faced with a dilemma: how much to attribute to the designer, how much to the architect? Or, from a broader viewpoint, how to bring together the diverse expressive aspects which are autonomous only at first sight?

These questions, and especially the development of the artist-craftsman (so pertinent in the case of Rietveld), and the intellectual growth of the man to the time of his complete maturity as an architect who was always able to find a suitable answer to the known problems of contemporary social production, are thoroughly examined in this study by Daniele Baroni, conducted with the skill we have come to associate with this historian of design and visual communication.

The historical detail and factual analysis contained in this study will enable the reader to follow all the experiences undergone by the architect during the ten to thirty years of his life—the time when he was part of the new movement—in his designs, interiors, and the private and public buildings which usually appear in many works of history and criticism as creations emerging spontaneously in the tradition of architectural practice in those years—recognizing Rietveld's participation in the De Stijl movement as a period of more intense activity—and at the same time which permitted him to become aware of all the important factors which I believe represent the basis of his renowned genius.

Filippo Alison

In this photograph Rietveld is seated on his new chair, constructed out of quadrangular listels, in front of his workshop in Adriaan van Ostadelaan, Utrecht, surrounded by his assistants. This photograph is an important biographical document; its date is uncertain, but was probably 1917. The boy leaning on the chair is Gerard van de Groenekan, Rietveld's future assistant. De Stijl was not yet officially in existence, and Mondrian had not yet expressed his theory of neoplasticism in painting. But with this chair Rietveld already expressed symbolically the spatial structure which became identified with the De Stijl conception of form, and at the same time he formulated his first eloquent manifesto.

An early photograph of Rietveld, published in De Stijl. nos. 79-84, 1927; a photograph taken when he was aged about sixty; G. van de Groenekan at work, 1974.

Before defining the methodological criteria adopted in the present study, it must be stated that in the work of Rietveld not everything can be documented, and it has not always been possible to reach a clear definition or an understanding of how certain events and episodes actually developed. On more than one occasion it has been necessary to have recourse to logical supposition. Rietveld himself, when he was asked, was not always able to give an accurate dating of his earlier work, nor has he left us an orderly and well-classified documentation. In fact, it seems likely that a shortage of studio space more than once led him to destroy documentary material which would undoubtedly have been valuable to students of his work. This suspicion is also voiced in the biography by Theodore M. Brown[1] who was in a position to collect direct evidence from Rietveld himself and whose critical acumen associated with historical rigor has made his biography a work of reference essential to anyone who takes an interest in Rietveld. In his designs of furniture and objects Rietveld hardly ever used the method of drawing up a plan at the drawing board but worked directly with the material, perhaps employing notes and rough sketches which were of use almost exclusively to his own interpretation. (This way of working marked a contrast to the methodological rigor of neoplasticism.) As a result of his continuous experimentation, we have more than one prototype of the same article, differing in dimensions or materials. In other cases, the craftsmen who worked together with him or reconstructed his designs at a later stage, with the exception of the faithful Gerard A. van de Groenekan, helped to make a difficult situation worse still by interpreting Rietveld's ideas according to the needs of the time and giving an incorrect rendering of more than one object.

In the present study the criterion which has been adopted for the reconstruction of objects has been to refer wherever possible to the original prototype, for both the dimensions and the materials employed, and to take into serious consideration only those variants which Rietveld himself thought definitive for possible production in the future. This has been achieved mainly because of the careful preservation of many of the prototypes in the Design Department of the Stedelijk Museum in Amsterdam.

Invaluable aids to a deeper understanding of the objects and the documentation they produced were the retrospective exhibitions of Rietveld's work held at the Centraal Museum, Utrecht, in 1958, and more recently at the Stedelijk Museum in November 1971. A great deal of the documentation which is available to us today is due to the constant presence by the side of Rietveld of Truus Schröder-Schräder, an architect who worked together with Rietveld from 1921 onward and who is the owner and curator of the museum-house which bears her name, the Schröder Huis.

But the person who perhaps more than any other worked most closely with Rietveld in his furniture activity was G. A. van de Groenekan who, in 1916–17 when still a young boy, entered his studio and has continued throughout his life to reproduce the most famous pieces for museums and private collectors all over the world.

In the pages which follow 68 objects created by Rietveld are presented, covering his whole activity in the sphere of furniture making. Of these, 36 are reconstructed in prototype or already form part of the mass-production process. The drawings which accompany them, here published in the scale of 1:10, serve as graphic notes leading to a clearer comprehension of the architectonic sign. There then follow descriptive notes containing the specific bibliography of the object (no account has been taken of the many reviews of the various exhibitions which have taken place from time to time), the exhibitions in which the object has appeared, and its place in a public or private collection.

[1] Theodore M. Brown, *The Work of G. Rietveld, Architect* (Cambridge, 1958).

Explanatory Note

Trademark of the furniture workshop on Adriaan van Ostadelaan.

11

Introduction:
Analysis of the Neoplastic Style

De Stijl arose as an artistic movement in reaction to the "domination of the baroque in modern architecture," and, by implication, to offer an alternative to the School of Amsterdam which was composed of a group of architects who gravitated around the journal *Wendingen* and represented the official architecture of the Netherlands. In this polemical position, so closely linked to the events of daily life and so "normal" for a movement of the avant-garde, De Stijl became the moving force which was to set in motion one of the most significant renewals of artistic thought in this century; even though, as we shall see, the neoplastic experiment was to remain incomplete.

But if we compare the two movements, De Stijl and Wendingen, in their attitudes toward architectural matters during the years before 1920, we can see that although they developed two opposing conceptions, both groups possessed a single cultural origin: both De Stijl and Wendingen were influenced by Berlage and Wright, the former group drawing inspiration from the rationalist and universal part of the message of these two masters, the latter developing the more imaginative, expressionistic, and individualistic side of their thought.

At times these two tendencies developed along parallel lines and appeared integrated in the expressive language of architects belonging to one or the other movement, to such a degree that their labels of identity could be interchanged, as was the case with Wils, Dudok, Staal, Duiker, and Bijvoet for example.[1] This can be explained also in the light of certain characteristics which were common to all Dutch architecture produced during those years.[2]

First and foremost, as we have seen, the formulation of the architectonic style of the two groups derived from the teaching of Berlage and the works of Wright. One must not overlook the common interest of Dutch artists (and of Wright) in Eastern architecture, Japanese in particular; the sense of geometry, firmly established in all Dutch architecture; the continuous flow of internal spaces as a common component; and the use of new materials alongside the more traditional ones.

It was not until painters, sculptors, and architects joined together to form De Stijl that the group showed its determination to shake off other cultural influences, stressing forcefully its opposition to all the art which preceded it.

"The old culture, the culture of Jean-Jacques Rousseau, the culture of the heart, the uncultured culture of the petty-bourgeois intelligenzia and its long-haired apostles Morris and Ruskin, the concentric culture, the culture of 'I' and 'mine,' is not yet quite dead"[3] inveighed Van Doesburg.

And at the same time De Stijl began to develop those concepts of modulation, de-composition, color, and transparency which formed the basis of a new art and took the group far away forever from any other tendency operating at the time.

Manifesto of the Movement[4]
1.   There exist an old and a new awareness of the period. The old tends to the individual. The new tends to the universal. The struggle between the individual and the universal is revealed in both the world war and contemporary art.
2.   War is now destroying the old world and what it contains: individual domination from all points of view.
3.   The new art has shown the content of the new awareness of our period: equal proportions of the individual and the universal.
4.   The new awareness of the epoch is ready to manifest itself in everything, even in the exterior life.
5.   The traditions, dogmas, and prerogatives of the individual (that which is natural) are opposed to this realization.

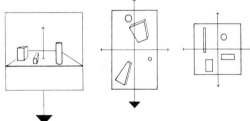

Diagram of the direction of gravity according to Rietveld: in the Renaissance, in the Cubist period; in De Stijl.

6.   The purpose of the journal *De Stijl* is to appeal to all who believe in the reform of art and culture to reject everything which impedes their development, as has been done by its collaborators by creating a new plastic art and suppressing the natural form which contradicts the very expression of art, the highest consequence of all artistic awareness.

7.   Contemporary artists have participated in the war which the world is waging on a spiritual plane, urged on by one and the same idea against the prerogatives of individualism: the caprice. They unite with all those who fight for the formation of a single international movement in Life, in Art, in Culture, both intellectual and material.

8.   *De Stijl*, founded for this purpose, is striving to bring this new idea of life into being.

The Sense of Geometry

The presence of painters in the group became a determining factor in its development. The future achievements of neoplastic architecture had first to pass through the pictorial phase. The school which served as a model for the De Stijl painters in the early stages was cubism. As is well known, the first generally accepted idea which the cubists contested and completely demolished was that of "perspective." People had become accustomed to observing the world in the Renaissance manner, adopting a three-dimensional view of it. Cubism introduced the concept of simultaneity into painting—a trend pursued at the same time by the futurists also—and this unknowingly led to the artistic representation of a scientific discovery of enormous importance and far-reaching effects at the beginning of the century: space-time, in other words, the fourth dimension.

It was the mathematician Minkowski who in 1908 first conceived the idea of a four-dimensional world: "Henceforth space by itself, and time by itself, are doomed to fade away into mere shadows, and only a kind of union of the two will preserve an independent reality."[5] The plane became the pictorial—and later architectural—expression of the fourth dimension.

For Mondrian, Van Doesburg, and Van der Leck, but for Huszar and Rietveld as well, the plane became identified with the new element of plasticity which was to be the starting point for the construction of the new art. The pictorial plane was to be thought of as no more than a point of departure. The further development of neoplasticism occurred when the path followed by cubism was finally abandoned in favor of pure abstraction, when an attempt was made to eliminate from the picture the "subject," and not only the subject but any form which could be taken to represent a subject or any kind of natural form. As Mondrian later wrote: "I came to realize that cubism did not draw the logical consequences of its own discoveries; it did not develop abstraction up to its ultimate end—the expression of pure reality."[6]

This same attempt to achieve expressive purification had been begun as early as 1915 by some Russian painters, especially Malevich who formulated the supremacist theory some years later. Malevich was the first artist to eliminate the subject from his compositions, arriving at the expression of pure nonobjectivity. He was the first to create a situation of interdependence between the plane and the formal elements which develop inside it—in nearly all cases dynamic rectangles—and which represented solely experiments in spatialsim. But from the very first the De Stijl painters aimed at the definition of a precise stylistic code and the attainment of a result which, by means of plastic elements, would eliminate any form of individual expression. The rectangular abstracts and structures based on straight lines which they adopted were at first based on standard-sized grill patterns which were already fairly widespread in studies of architectural geometry in Holland, due especially to the work of De Groot, who was the greatest scholar in this field. Or, they may perhaps have been influenced by the *Quadratum en Triangulatur* of Berlage, or looking further afield, as can be seen in the paintings, to the geometry emerging from

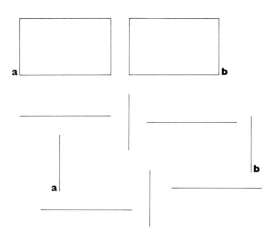

T. van Doesburg, plan of closed-in geometrical forms and relative neoplastic de-composition.

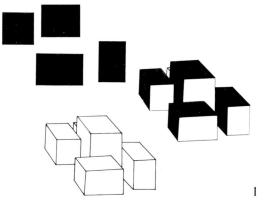

T. van Doesburg, composition in painting (form, time, color); sculpture (space, time, line, plane, volume); architecture (space, time, line, plane).

13

14

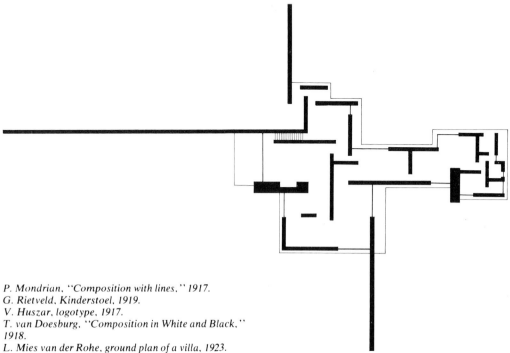

P. Mondrian, ''Composition with lines,'' 1917.
G. Rietveld, Kinderstoel, 1919.
V. Huszar, logotype, 1917.
T. van Doesburg, ''Composition in White and Black,''
1918.
L. Mies van der Rohe, ground plan of a villa, 1923.

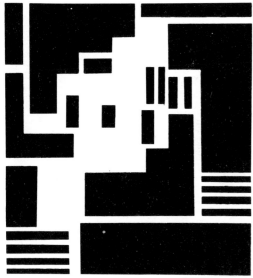

V. Huszar, cover of De Stijl, *1917.*

T. van Doesburg and C. van Eesteren,
''Counter-construction,''1920, axonometry.

H. Richter, ''Filmmoment,'' 1923.

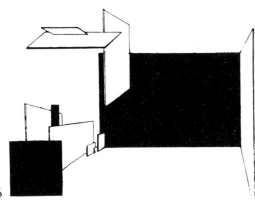

the standard-sized architecture of ancient Japan. For these reasons it can be understood that even before they came to know each other the De Stijl painters were already predisposed to work along similar lines, even if, in the words of Jaffé, "the event—that is, the attainment of their common orientation—must be considered as a moment of spiritual short-circuit among several persons."[7]

Even at the time of the Dutch art nouveau many artists had evinced a particular interest in the geometrical-mathematical root and a study of proportional values. Various studies of the theory of form were current even in the first years of the century. Architectural decoration, graphics, interior design, and textiles were all based on geometrical research in those years. Jaffé relates this innate Dutch sense of geometry to a psychical affinity with the artifical landscape of the country, which is all horizontal, with the various composed elements of the technological culture emerging out of it in a vertical direction. I believe this interpretation should be considered very marginal, although there is no doubt that it does contain an element of truth. Geometrical analysis taken to its extreme consequences, to the attainment of the neoplastic essence, resulted from an internal debate, both individual and as a group, rather than from any natural unconscious element.

Using only the primary plastic elements: the straight line, the right angle, the rectangle, and the colors yellow, red, blue (primary colors), white, gray, and black (neutral colors), the De Stijl painters formed the structural syntax which was automatically translated into the theory of neoplasticism.

The horizontal and vertical determine the right angle, that is the "typical angle," one of the elements they brought to perfection. As Mondrian said, "I found that the right angle is the only constant relationship and that through the proportion of the dimensions one can confer movement, that is, life, to its immutable expression."[8] And again, "Where lines cross or touch each other tangentially, without for this reason ceasing to continue."[9] For a mathematical equation, the De Stijl artists simplified every element of the composition until only one was left, the basic structure of equilibrium, and eliminated from their visual "equation" everything which was inessential so as to reach a new visual conception.

In reality De Stijl was the last challenge—operated from within—to elementary Euclidean geometry. It was a challenge made by means of the same instruments which led to classical and academic art and which helped to establish the mathematical concept of the "golden." In this case it was to attain a universal "equilibrium," which is merely another way of saying "harmony" according to the classical concept of beauty. However, in this ideal of universal equilibrium there is an interpretation which was similar to the views of Theosophy and Utopianism, and, as we shall see later, this was to imprint a special character onto it. Furthermore, it must not be forgotten that neoplastic analysis came to be identified with the essential ideas of *Gestaltung*, and it was this which became the new aspect leading to the formulation of a theory of vision.

According to psychological theories which were not set down until a later date, it is known now, but was not then, that a network of open lines leads to various directions in space, creating a suspended optical construction: a dynamic spatial construction. Each linear unit has a kinetic inertia, tending to prolong itself in the same direction and with the same movement. The vitality of an equilibrium depends on the entity of the opposing forces which balance each other.[10] "When two lines cross, the fields of force struggle and the spatial energies are concentrated on the reflecting angle."[11] The delimitation of the pictorial field acts as a screen to transform the optical impulses into spatial forces, which will enable the latter to be transmuted into plastic forces by way of a physiological and psychic process. These new visual concepts which were understood by the neoplastic

G. Vantongerloo, plastic construction, 1919.

G. Rietveld, Berlijnse stoel, 1923.

17

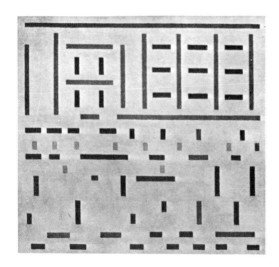

B. van der Leck, "Geometrical Composition," 1917.

P. Mondrian, "Composition with Gray Lines," 1919.

T. van Doesburg, "Russian Dance," 1918.

De Stijl Painting: The Dutch Period

painters proved exceptionally important to architects in their spatial studies and were the first step in the organization of the spatial world and of the sense of dimension.

As Van Doesburg said: "In the figurative use of the straight line stands the awareness of a new culture."[12] Argan referred to this subject in these words: "The point of arrival or stopping, in Mondrian's formal analysis: the point at which, when perception and form are superimposed and identified one with the other (or one and the other being equivalent to zero), no further formal process remains possible."[13] This is the identification of a *Gestaltstheorie.*

The Concept of Order

Whatever the human mind wishes to understand, order is an indispensable condition for this understanding.[14] The sense of order, seen as a process of mental and physiological organization, is innate in man, but there are various systems of order and many kinds of experiences and applications. Much space divides the Platonic conception of order from the "psychophysical isomorphism" defined by Gestalt psychology.

What, then, is the meaning of "order" in art? How could it be understood and in what could it be identified in De Stijl, even if the term were frequently replaced by the more symbolical "equilibrium"? Let us attempt to interpret the concept of order as it was understood by the members of De Stijl.

After all, as Monroe C. Beardsley suggested, a long tradition with roots in Greek philosophy, which has never been entirely overthrown, describes art as principally or entirely engaged in the production of order, harmony, proportion, etc.[15] And this cannot have failed to be the point of departure for Mondrian and the others. But to have made the search for a universal order their highest objective presupposes that for De Stijl order meant something more than the order understood by the ancient Greeks.

Today the psychological sciences show us geometrical order displayed in opposition to mechanical disorder (the principle of entropy), and order can be analysed by means of the same instruments used in Gestalt psychology, which has sufficient means of determining levels of complexity and regularity.

According to Arnheim, physicists speak of entropy as a tendency to disorder, when they concentrate on the catabolic destruction of form. In contrast, Gestalt theorists concentrate on situations where a disordered or relatively less ordered constellation of forces is free and at the same time constrained to assume a greater order.[16]

But if it is true that perfection is a situation of order and calm, as in the order of utopias and cosmologies, this does not mean that a high level of structural order is a sufficient precondition for the production of art.

Let us see what Mondrian and Van Doesburg said about this. "Equilibrium and perfection are more essential than form and object. If it is possible to arrive at the creation of a work of art, using only these two superior qualities, I ask myself what 'usefulness' such factors as 'form' and 'object' can have."[17] The rigorous analysis of the foundations of plastic expression was therefore based on equilibrium. As Jaffé wrote, "the entire grammatical structure of formal style is founded on the research into *equilibrium*, so as to obtain it 'chemically pure.'"[18] In order to obtain it in this form, the De Stijl painters tried to organize space into a carefully measured relationship between lines and colors. It was the *relationship* defined by Mondrian which represented the secret of this equilibrium; a purely plastic expression was created out of relationships of line, plane, and color, so arriving at harmony in opposition to chaos. "In the art of the past *relationships were veiled and confused* because they were subordinated to natural form."[19] And again: "The more neutral are the plastic means, the more possible is it to determine the immutable expression of reality. We can consider as relatively neutral those forms which show no relationship with the natural appearance of things or with some kind of 'idea.' Abstract forms or de-composed parts of forms, can be considered relatively neutral."[20] Neutral forms could organize a state of calm, enabling the artist to express a universal iconographic language, a new language which would be impersonal and intelligible to everyone, "so that there should come out of it an entirely new way of seeing and thinking."[21] Concerning the other element which contributes to the formulation of the creative syntax, that is, the straight line, we read: "The absolute is expressed through the medium of the straight line. Painting and architecture, according to the new aesthetics, are the coherent expression of a composition built on straight lines, neutralized, and therefore

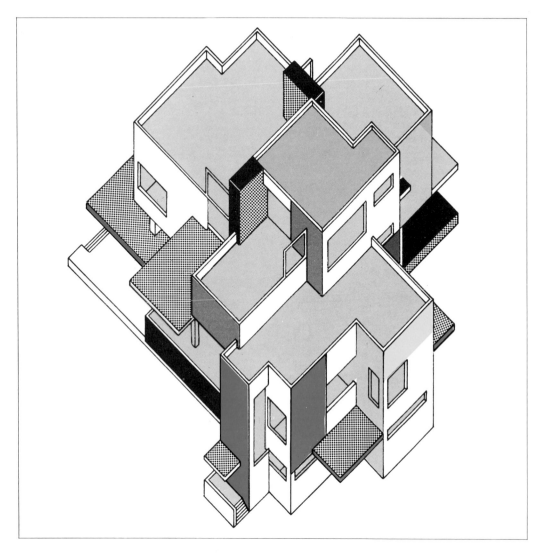

On the left: *T. van Doesburg and C. van Eesteren,
design for a private house, 1920, axonometry;* above:
*C. van Eesteren, design for a house on the river, 1923;
T. van Doesburg and C. van Eesteren, studio-house for
an artist, 1923, model;* below: *T. van Doesburg and C.
van Eesteren, hotel for Léonce Rosenberg, 1923; two
views of the model created by Rietveld.*

De Stijl Architecture: The Theoretical Phase

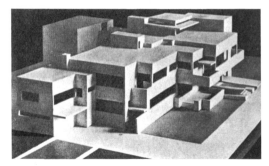

with a multiple repetition of the dualism of the unchangeable rectangular position."[22]
A further characteristic of De Stijl was its constant dualism—derived from Platonic dualism—which was seen as a dichotomy or opposition, always producing a state of tension. Thus there occurred a struggle, confrontation, or mutual exclusion between: abstraction and nature; the objective and the subjective; order and chaos; form and matter; the dynamic and the static; symmetry and asymmetry; space-time and three-dimensionalism; horizontal and vertical; color and neutral; yellow and blue.
In their search for abstraction, for a sublime relationship of all the plastic elements, for the attainment of truth by way of a universal vision, and the finding of relationships of balance and perfection, the De Stijl artists came very close to the ideas expressed in Platonism. While they mirrored to a large extent the ideal of beauty held by the ancient Greeks, this was expressed in modern radical terms, and some ingredients of Nordic thought, as well as the results of other avant-garde experimentation, became superimposed onto this ideal.

Philosophical Components
In the thought of De Stijl, therefore, the findings of modern science were superimposed onto the philosophical ideas held by the ancients, notably Aristotle and Plato. As we have seen, De Stijl was based on the principle of order, identifying disorder with chaos, a synonym for sorrow. The ultimate aim of art, according to Mondrian, is "the elimination of the tragic." In his view the elimination of the tragic element from the life of mankind was the specific task of art, since tragedy, sorrow, and anguish were formed out of the morbid atmosphere produced by what is formless, irrational, or incomplete. Developing a purely plastic vision, he added: "Only the man who has learnt how to transpose what is individual into the universal will escape the tragic emotion."[23] Even sentiment would

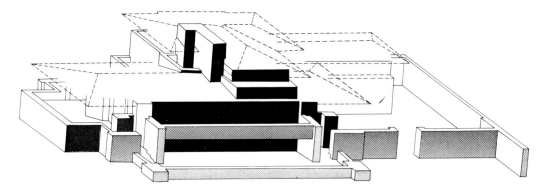

Analysis of the composition of the volumes and planes in a house by Frank Lloyd Wright, according to R. B. Tague.

have no place in art since it too could become a cause of sorrow, as could emotion, contemplation, and everything which could lead to a metaphysical outcome. "Any kind of emotion, whether of sorrow or joy, implies a breach in the harmony and equilibrium between the *subject* (man) and the *object* (the universe). The work of art must create for itself an equilibrium with the universe; feelings and emotions lead to a state exactly opposed to this."[24] And again Mondrian declared: "Immutable, equilibrium is beyond all sorrow and all joy."[25]
These ideas were closely connected with the platonic ideal which was interpreted by Mondrian's friend Schoenmaekers who was engaged in a study of philosophical and theosophical problems. He was also the author of two fundamental works for an understanding of the thought of De Stijl: *Het nieuwe wereldbeeld* (1915)[26] and *Beginselen der beeldende wiskunde* (1916).[27]

Exhibition of De Stijl in the Galerie L'Effort Moderne. Paris, 1923.

C. van Eesteren and T. van Doesburg at work in Paris, 1923: photo published in De Stijl, nos. 6, 7, 1924.

Some of the concepts expressed by Mondrian, and apparently formulated also by Schoenmaekers, can be found in Plato's *Philebus*. To give an example, we can quote some footnotes to Plato's work by Nicola Abbagnano: "Pleasure and sorrow belong to the sphere of that which is without limit: in themselves they have neither limit nor measure. . . . Out of the union of the unlimited and the limit, that is, out of the function which the limit exercises over the multiple by reducing it to unity, is born the *mixed genus*. The mixed genus is therefore the order of the multiple, the proportion of quantity, the harmony of variety. Everything in the world and in mankind which is order, proportion, harmony, everything which has measure and number, belongs to the mixed genus. . . . So that between sorrow and pleasure there is room for a third state, which is that of indifference, the state in fact of the intelligence. . . . The mixed genus comprises everything which has order and harmony both in the world and in the mind of man. It is a *genesis directed toward the essence*, that is, a development tending to represent the being in its state of perfection. . . . The nature of good, therefore, lies in proportion and order which guarantee the truth and beauty of life in its many facets. Measure and order, therefore, belong by their nature to the eternal, that is, to the absolute being."[28]

All Mondrian's thought was closely connected to the neoplatonism of Schoenmaekers, enriched by overtones of the secret theosophical symbolism in which he too was a believer. This certainly represented an enormous contradiction, an unstable balance between the mathematical certainty of the rational and the limitless world of the supernatural. But Mondrian adapted this cosmic conception in the manner of the great philosophers of the past who were at one and the same time mathematicians and astronomers, in a union between numbers and stars, just in the same way as the Theosophical, Anthroposophical, and Rosacrucian movements tried to surpass the limits set by time and space to pursue the notion of structure in the universe.

Schoenmaekers succeeded in fusing mysticism and universality, identifying this universal force in the "Stijl," and this was the reason for his influence over Mondrian and the others. "Plastic mathematics must be identified with exact and methodical thought on the part of the creator. Plastic mathematics signifies: a vigilant and uninterrupted awareness of love nurtured by the person who creates for the object of his creation, so that he is able to contemplate his creation with a degree of prudence equal to that love."[29] And again: "Truth means: reducing the relativity of natural factors to the absolute, so as to rediscover the absolute in natural factors."[30] Though somewhat personal and tortuous, these theories did set in motion Mondrian's speculations into plasticity. He derived from the writings of his philosopher friend the content of his work as well as his positivist attitude toward the world. Even the expression *nieuwe beelding*, which Mondrian made widely known, originated with Schoenmaekers. For both men a determining factor was their membership in the Theosophical Society, which in those years had branches in all parts of the westen world.[31] Theosophists place great importance on the geometrical element, although for the most part they value it for its symbolic quality. Unlike the German expressionists belonging to the circle of Bruno Taut whose research was founded on the triangular element and the pyramid, so penetrating deep into the symbolic values of Theosophical concepts, the De Stijl artists confined themselves to the use of the straight line and rectangle. But here the symbolic value of bipolarity came in, with the vertical element corresponding to the masculine and the horizontal to the feminine. Mondrian himself expressed this idea in one of his equations: "vertical = masculine = space = statics = harmony; horizontal = feminine = time = dynamics = melody."[32]

The same idea was emphasized by Schoenmaekers: "Contraries always appear in a relationship one with the other which can be reduced to the relationship between the active and passive; for example, 'male' and 'female' are contraries, but not opposites. . . . The two basic, radical, contraries on which the earth and all that is on the earth are modelled, are the horizontal line of energy, or the orbit of the earth around the sun, and the vertical movement, of an essentially spatial nature, of the rays which originate in the centre of the sun."[33]

It is clear how great an importance was attributed to the geometrical sign which was superimposed onto the cosmic meanings of the universe. Yet even if Mondrian was alone in accepting the indoctrination of the Theosophists, there was a broad convergence of all the aspects of thought which constituted the De Stijl credo, even on the part of artists whose early influences had been quite different. Vantongerloo, who was as a sculpture came from a different background and tried to reduce all his work to mathematical equations, wrote: "Philosophy speaks of a point, a line, a plane, a volume, it speaks of light and color, for the purpose of explaining the universe. The scientist uses these same means to reveal the cosmos as a new force. The artist again employs the same means to unveil the splendor of the cosmos. Philosophy, science, and art, through evolution, tend to unity."[34]

Van Doesburg's links with theosophy were very marginal, and his first approach to the spiritual life was through Kandinsky's *The Spiritual in Art* and later through Mondrian. With his dogmatic bent, he appears to us today more directly a Hegelian; but he too was in perfect agreement with Mondrian concerning the universal and constant value of art as a guide to harmony. In neoplasticism he saw the plastic manifestation of the laws formulated by Hegel, and his theory of *de nieuwe beelding* is a further development of the ideas contained in *The Spiritual in Art*, which was to some extent based on Hegelian doctrine. As he wrote in 1918: "In purely abstract thought every emotional associative perception (naturalistic) is absent and in their place are relations between ideas. This idea may be represented in an exact mathematical figure, as occurs in mathematics proper, with numbers. In this type of representation the notion and content of pure thought become visible. And in this case, where the content of pure thought becomes an image (*beelding*), we have already a plastic contemplation (*beeldende*)."[35]

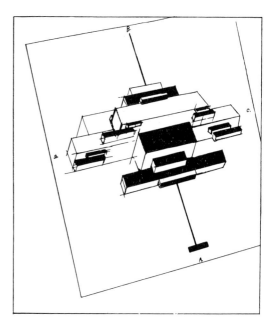

K. Malevich, "Unovis." Design for the future Zemljaniti, 1924.

The rationalism of Descartes, in his *Discours de la méthode*, and of Spinoza, especially in the *Ethics*, were obviously another part of the De Stijl cultural heritage, but more than anything else it was the Dutch tradition of thought which cemented the principles of the group. To use a term which was coined by Huizinga and later became famous, it was the *Nederlands geestesmerk*, or the trademark of the Dutch spirit. In fact, even the political life of the country was dominated by theological currents and the political parties based their ideals on spiritual convictions. At this point one should not overlook the iconoclastic tendency of Protestantism, founded on a rigidly universalistic doctrine which held, as Jaffé wrote, that "every representation of the divine in the form of creation constituted a sacrilege and was therefore anathema. The strength of the universalistic conception of De Stijl and its aversion to all forms of personalism could almost be compared with the Protestant faith of the sixteenth century."[36]

In their rejection of all that is natural and their abolition of any kind of subject, the iconoclastic doctrines of Protestantism were partly accepted and assimilated by De Stijl. "It is as wrong to identify the essence of thought in contemplation as to identify it in the actual representation of nature. The latter is a concept of classical and Roman Catholic origin, which has always been contested by Protestantism."[37]

Toward a New Relationship Between the Artist and Society
Their search for perfection, equilibrium, pure relationships, order, and the universal did not restrict De Stijl to problems of art and philosophy, but tended to encompass the whole

H. Arp, *painted staircase in the cabaret Aubette, Strasbourg, 1928.*

system of life and all the aspects which produce it, starting with the environment in which man lives.

The utopian vision of the world held by Mondrian and the other members of the group was without a doubt still a romantic, or more precisely, philosophical vision, but it differed from all other nineteenth-century utopian concepts since it was founded essentially on an aesthetic idea rather than on social and political principles, even though, just because of their universal nature, the latter contained a strong sense of collectivism. We are still far away from the forms of regeneration of art through revolution, as exemplified by many Russian and German artists, and far too from such other utopian tendencies as that of a "cosmic communism" followed by the expressionist circle of Bruno Taut.

The striving for a universal and collective style already formed the basis of a utopian attitude which was the first step toward a turning to life. In his *New Life* Mondrian says: "For the new man, the universal is not a vague idea, but a living reality which is manifested visibly and audibly."[38] And again: "The pure plastic vision must construct a new society, as in art it has constructed a new expression: a society founded on an equilibrium of the dualism between mind and matter, a society of well-balanced relationships."[39] Thus De Stijl postulated the relationship between art and life which it founded on perfection of style. Jaffé wrote: "The whole development of De Stijl and neoplasticism is based on the evolution of life and the attitude of man toward his environment, and the development of art is parallel to the evolutionary line of life. Not only parallel: it must be first of all the plastic expression of the new trends whose mark has been imprinted on contemporary life."[40]

This natural development occurred when the lyricism of pure abstraction was left behind and artists turned their attention to designing for the neoplastic environment, abandoning the plane surface of the picture for the dimensional development of architecture.

In order to understand and describe this new relationship between artist and society according to De Stijl, we must return for a moment to the period of determining importance for the growth of a social conscience in art, that is, to the first years of this century, and examine the differing views of this concept given by two Dutch masters: De Bazel and Berlage. The former had no doubts in espousing the cause of "individual progress" and following a traditionalist orientation; he did not believe in the possibility of a radical change in style. It was no accident that the *Wendingen* group became identified with his thought. Berlage, on the other hand, had from the beginning of the century shared the ideas of Muthesius, and had made them widely known in his own country. Aligning himself with the other international early-rationalist artists, he expressed a firm belief in the social function of art and was one of the first to discuss the ideas contained in the *Nieuwe zakelijkheid*, with its adherence to objectivity which later became such a firm plank of the rationalist platform. De Stijl was formed according to the teaching of Berlage. "The urge to collectivism is manifested to a high degree in social life; autocracy, imperialism with its "natural" law of the strongest, are about to collapse, if they have not done so already, to make way for the spiritual powers of the law."[41] The subordination of the individual to the collective became an integral part of the De Stijl program; but at this stage it was as a purely spiritual thought, a kind of philosophical socialism mixed with anarchy, similar to the idea previously expressed by theosophy.

To some extent this was due to the fact that in the first decades of the century spiritual and theological tendencies still played an important part in Dutch social and political life. No political party existed which represented the interests of any particular social class. To quote Jaffé again: "This unswerving fidelity to a law which has not been manifestly revealed, but which man's conscience must rediscover each time, is essentially Protestant in nature; and it is an aspect which frequently recurs in the history of the Netherlands and is closely connected to the importance placed by the Dutch tradition on the individual conscience."[42]

From this time onward Mondrian, Van Doesburg, and the others worked for the future, for the men of the future, convinced that in the values of plasticity were to be found the solutions to all the moral and social problems of the new society. For the reasons we have seen, even problems relating to social class were viewed by purely aesthetic criteria, thus placing them in the same utopian dimension that has been identified on previous occasions.

Van Doesburg has interpreted "proletariat and bourgeoisie" as follows: "No art of the proletariat exists, because when once the proletariat has created art, it ceases to be a proletariat and becomes an artist. The artist is neither proletarian nor bourgeois and what he has created belongs neither to the proletariat nor to the bourgeoisie; it belongs to everyone. Art is a spiritual activity of man whose purpose is to liberate him from the chaos of life, and from tragedy. Art is free in the application of its means, but is limited by its own laws and by nothing else. As soon as a work becomes a work of art, it surpasses by far the class differences between proletariat and bourgeoisie. . . . Art as we postulate it is neither proletarian nor bourgeoisie. It develops forces sufficiently efficacious to enable it to influence all culture instead of being influenced in its turn by social relationships."[43]

And in the words of Mondrian: "The most urgent task is to guarantee mankind an independent existence in both the material and immaterial fields of life, and it is to this task that we must dedicate ourselves above all. The New Life will not liberate man if man does not continually civilize individual and reciprocal relationships."[44]

The next step in the new life was to imagine the new city. De Stijl believed in the development of the metropolis, rather than the rural life and static landscape which belonged to the nineteenth century; just as they believed in the machine and in technical and scientific progress.

"At present neoplasticism shows in painting what will one day surround us in the form of architecture and sculpture."[45] De Stijl lacked the breadth of vision which could develop the neoplastic city. Or at any rate, the group did not produce any plans similar to those of Sant'Elia for the futurist city or of Le Corbusier for *La Ville Radieuse*. Van Doesburg's city of traffic was an unexceptional project, only partly resolved: it lacked that element of genius which could have made it exceptional. The most important aspect of De Stijl urban design remains without a doubt the "mental project," the "urban dream" (in Zevi's definition) of Mondrian, where once again absolute equilibrium was sought as the only path to salvation.

"The truly evolved human being will no longer attempt to cultivate, protect, or beautify streets and parks with flowers and trees, *but will construct healthy and beautiful cities by means of a well-balanced contrast between buildings and empty spaces*. The exterior will give him just as much satisfaction as the interior. . . .

"As long as man is dominated by individualism, and neglects to cultivate his universal essence, he does not seek nor can he find his own person. The house too becomes the place where this fleeting individuality is cultivated, and its plastic expression reflects this trivial preoccupation. *The exteriorization of this self-centeredness has been fatal to the whole period*. In order to attain a pure and therefore healthy and practical beauty, it is necessary for our physical environment no longer to be the outflow of our wretched personality and no longer to contain a lyrical expression, but its contrary, which is purely plastic. . . .

"Neoplasticism is responsible for *replacing lyricism with pure plasticity*. Through a

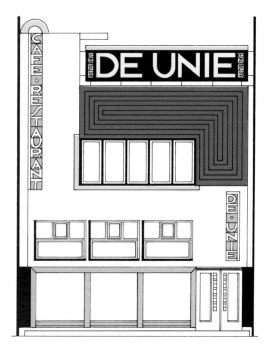

J. J. P. Oud, "Café Unie," Rotterdam, 1925.

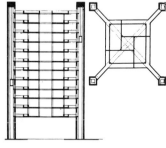

T. van Doesburg, skyscrapers in the "City of Traffic," 1929.

studied but variable rhythm in the relationships of an almost mathematical plastic means, this art can almost attain to the superhuman, and certainly the universal. This is possible, already today, since art precedes life. In realizing itself in life through the creation of our physical environment, neoplastic art loses some of its superhuman character, but still reveals enough of it for the individual no longer to feel himself an insignificant being but be uplifted toward universal life through the medium of beauty.

"*The pure and logical plastic concept is always in accord with practical requirements*, the question is one of equilibrium. Our period (the future!) requires pure equilibrium and there is only one way it can find it. There are infinite ways of expressing beauty, but the pure way, that is, the expression of equilibrium, is manifested only through the expressive means of pure plasticity. This is one of the most important laws of neoplasticism applying to the construction of the house, street, or city. But pure methods in themselves do not engender neoplastic expression: *they must be composed in such a way that they lose their individuality so that, in a neutralizing and nullifying opposition, they come to form an indivisible unity.* . . .

"In architecture, matter is denaturalized in various ways, and technology has not yet said the final word on this matter. *Ruggedness, a rustic appearance* (typical of natural materials) *must disappear.* Therefore:
1. The surface of the materials will be smooth and shining, so diminishing their heaviness. Once again neoplastic art is in accord with hygiene which requires smooth and easily cleaned surfaces.
2. The natural color of the materials must also disappear, so far as possible, beneath a layer of pure color or noncolor.
3. Not only the material as a plastic means (a constructive element) will be denaturalized, but also architectural composition. *The natural structure will be nullified by neutralizing contrasts.*

"The application of these norms will destroy the tragic expression of the house, street, and city. By way of balanced contrasts, relationships of measurement (dimensions), and colors supported by relationships of position, a physical and moral joy will be generated which is the condition of health. With a little goodwill, it will not be impossible to create a kind of Eden. . . .

"I conclude: the house will no longer be enclosed, shut in, detached. Nor will the street. In spite of their different functions, these two elements must be unified. To this end one can no longer think of the house as a box or an empty space. The idea of a house—house dear house, home sweet home—must disappear, as must the idea of a 'street.'

"Like the city, we must consider the house and street as *a unity formed by planes composed of neutralizing contrasts which can nullify any kind of exclusivism.* The same principle is valid with regard to the interior of the house. No longer can it be a heap of pieces made up by four walls, with holes for doors and windows, but *a construction made up of infinite colored and noncolored planes in harmony, with furniture and objects which will be nothing in themselves, but will act as constructive elements of the whole.*

"And man? Being nothing in himself, he will be merely a part of the whole, and then, having lost the vanity of his small and trivial individuality, he will be happy in this Eden which he himself has *created*!"[46]

It is obvious that Mondrian's program has already incorporated the theoretical studies into neoplastic architecture undertaken by Van Doesburg after 1920 and pursued later by Van Eesteren and Rietveld also. This theoretical phase of De Stijl architecture existed in the period from 1920 to 1923 and culminated in the exhibition held in Léonce Rosenberg's Galerie L'Effort Moderne in Paris.

The house had been analyzed, sectioned, de-composed, and put together again in its plastic elements. The historical axis belonging to traditional construction had been destroyed. The house had been developed in each of its parts, on its four sides, above and below. This analytical method opened up new ways, new possibilities in building and design. After 1923 a movement "away from speculative reasoning to the experimental method" could be observed: Van Eesteren and Rietveld brought a new orientation to the speculation which had been purely utopian and turned it toward concrete realization. The journey from abstract theory to the new objectivity now seemed to have reached completion. Mondrian himself stated: "Since neoplasticism represents the realization of the principles of neoplastic painting in the whole environment which surrounds us, and especially in buildings, this already implies the start of attaining, in life, a more universal order. For this reason neoplasticism has its own cultural importance. Its concrete manifestation is convincing."[47]

The most significant evidence, and the first example of a residential nucleus of the future neoplastic city, was already a reality: Rietveld's 1924 Schröder Huis in Utrecht.

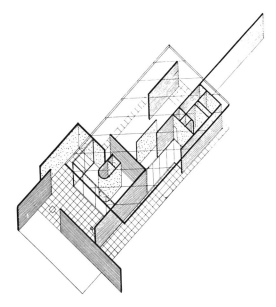

L. Mies van der Rohe, house shown in the Berlin exhibition, 1931.

[1] For a more detailed analysis of the relationship between the two movements and the activity of the individual architects mentioned, see Giovanni Fanelli, *Architettura moderna in Olanda* (Florence, 1968).

[2] Another curious factor was the fact that the two journals bore names which might appear interchangeable to the two movements: *Wendingen*, in fact, means "change of direction," and would seem more congenial to the Van Doesburg group.

[3] Published in *De Stijl*, II, 9 (July 1919).

[4] Published in *De Stijl*, II, 10 (November 1918), and signed by Theo van Doesburg, Robert van't Hoff, Vilmos Huszar, Antony Kok, Piet Mondrian, Georges Vantongerloo, and Jan Wils.

[5] Siegfried Giedion, *Space, Time, and Architecture* (Cambridge, Mass. 1941).

[6] Piet Mondrian, *Essays* (1930), Hans L. C. Jaffé, *De Stijl 1917-1931* (Amsterdam, 1956; Italian ed. Milan, 1964).

[7] Hans L.C. Jaffé, op. cit.

[8] Piet Mondrian, *Essays*.

[9] Piet Mondrian, *Le neoplasticisme* (1920).

[10] George Kepes, *Language of Vision* (Chicago, 1944; Italian ed. Bari, 1971).

[11] Ibid.

[12] Theo van Doesburg, in *De Stijl* (1927).

[13] Giulio Carlo Argan, *Gropius e la Bauhaus* (Turin, 1950).

[14] Rudolph Arnheim, *Entropy and Art: An Essay on Disorder and Order* (Berkeley, 1971).

[15] Monroe C. Beardsley, "Order and Disorder in Art" in Arnheim, op. cit.

[16] Rudolf Arnheim, op. cit.

[17] Theo van Doesburg, in *De Stijl* (1927).

[18] Hans L.C. Jaffé, op. cit.

[19] Piet Mondrian, *New Life* (1931). Quoted in Hans L.C. Jaffé, op. cit.

[20] Piet Mondrian, *Essays*, op. cit.

[21] Piet Mondrian, in *De Stijl*, VI, 1 (March 1923).

[22] Piet Mondrian, in *De Stijl*, VI, 5 (March 1923).

[23] Piet Mondrian, in *De Stijl*, II, 11 (September 1919).

[24] Theo van Doesburg, in *De Stijl*, V, 12 (December 1922).

[25] Piet Mondrian, *Neue Gestaltung* (Bauhausbücher: Munich, 1925).

[26] *The new image of the world.*

[27] *Principles of plastic mathematics.*

[28] Nicola Abbagnano, notes to *Philebus*, 2nd ed. (Turin, 1944).

[29] Schoenmaekers, *Beginselen der beeldende wiskunde*, op. cit.

[30] Schoenmaekers, *Het nieuwe wereldbeeld*, op. cit.

[31] The Theosophical Society was founded in 1875 by Helen Blavatsky, a Russian who claimed to have been initiated into it in Tibet and who exhibited psychic phenomena, supported by the guidance of the Mahatma.

[32] Piet Mondrian, quoted by Van Doesburg in *Neue Schweizer Rundschau* (1929).

[33] Schoenmaekers, *Het nieuwe wereldbeeld*. Quoted in Hans L.C. Jaffé, op. cit.

[34] Georges Vantongerloo, *L'art et son avenir* (1924). Quoted in Hans L.C. Jaffé, op. cit.

[35] Theo van Doesburg, in *De Stijl*, II, 2 (December 1918).

[36] Hans L.C. Jaffé, op. cit.

[37] Theo van Doesburg, in *De Stijl*, II, 2 (December 1918).

[38] Piet Mondrian, *Neue Gestaltung*.

[39] Piet Mondrian, in *De Stijl*, II, 12 (October 1919).

[40] Hans L.C. Jaffé, op. cit.

[41] Piet Mondrian, in *De Stijl*, I, 5 (March 1918).

[42] Hans L.C. Jaffé, op. cit.

[43] Theo van Doesburg, in *De Stijl*, VI, 2 (April 1923).

[44] Piet Mondrian, *New Life*. Quoted in Hans L.C. Jaffé, op. cit.

[45] Piet Mondrian, in *De Stijl*, III, 2 (December 1919).

[46] Piet Mondrian, "Man—street—city," in *i 10*, I (1927). Quoted in its entirety in Bruno Zevi, *Poetica dell'architettura neoplastica*, new edition (Turin 1974).

[47] Ibid.

Premise

To read a message according to the code on whose basis it was emitted is without a doubt the most logical aspect of serious research. To record this message in such a way that it appears as new as when it was first arrived at is the objective I set before myself here. When, as in our case, this message has remained almost unimpaired, and therefore not obsolete, we are put into the happy position of spectators, automatically enabled to participate in a reappraisal of this same message. The global assimilation of its mode of communication has better prepared us to interpret it without having to compromise by rejecting or only partially accepting some of its implications. This is made possible by the additional connotations we attribute to it on the basis of our understanding today (theory of the codes of enrichment).[1]

We have to investigate objects which always denote a primary function, but at the same time they have wide meanings and ideological connotations, extending far beyond simple function.

In addition, another aspect which is superimposed and interwoven with the former, is that of historical analysis, an examination of the social and cultural relations between the subject and the world which surrounds it. This is what I shall endeavor to undertake in the following pages.

The career of Rietveld began when he worked as a cabinetmaker, and although, as we shall see, he later chose architecture as his main activity, his youthful training was that of a craftsman in furniture. His roots were in popular art, but not in folk art, except during the most insecure period of his adolescence when his works were merely copies of the styles of the past. His constructions are elementary in structure, essential in form; their reflection of an archaic view of life is unmistakable. He rejected completely any kind of decoration or symbolical overtones and did not even identify himself with the cultural background of his native tradition. He went straight to the root of man's primary necessities, with origins in early history and primitive society.

By sheer historical coincidence, however, this way of considering the article of furniture happened to fit perfectly with the thought expressed in art by certain painters, architects, and writers of his own country, who were soon to join together to form the avant-garde movement which became known as De Stijl, whose style and thought have been analysed in the Introduction to this volume. Even if they worked according to different premises, Rietveld's approach to the object of furniture adopted the same system of signs that was used by the painters and the architects of the De Stijl group, of which he himself later became a member. In setting about making an article of furniture he did not question the basic logic of its function or concern himself with wider problems of housing, as Le Corbusier later did when he looked for a new meaning for certain objects in relation to others and put them forward as models for the life of the future. Rietveld confined himself to applying a different style to the known types of furniture which were part of the tradition of western civilization. He accepted this tradition and limited himself to imbuing the objects which had been in existence for a long time with a completely unexpected meaning. His contribution was exclusively one of style. "Our furniture, be it chairs, tables, or cupboards, represents the abstract-concrete objects of our future interiors."[2] His chairs remain chairs, his tables are always tables, but they contain new semantic values. This is why Rietveld must be considered a cabinetmaker rather than an architect and why his work is to be assigned mainly to the history of the great furniture makers. The artistic personality of Rietveld has been examined in the historical study by Siegfried Giedion who has attempted to provide a chronological account of the interrelationships over the years—from the Middle Ages onward—among the various craftsmen who created furniture: joiners, carpenters, cabinetmakers, decorators, upholsterers, mechanical engineers, until the historical avant-garde movements of the first two decades of this century declared that the new optics meant that the article of furniture must be perfectly integrated into the "new environment," to the extent that those among them who had begun by designing furniture were later seen to be architects too.[3] And this was true of Rietveld as well.

Of all forms of furniture Rietveld preferred the chair: this object undoubtedly presents stimulating architectural aspects, but presents considerable difficulty as well since what it is is an actual building on a reduced scale, incorporating the same rhythms, tensions, planes, structures, three-dimensionalism, and dynamics. This may be the reason for the predominance of the chair in the work of the great architects of the twentieth century, from Mackintosh to Wright, Le Corbusier, and Breuer. If instead of having been a furniture maker, designer, or architect, Rietveld had been a purely visual artist, these objects of his, these chairs, would have become autonomous spatial structures; his three-dimensional pattern based on Cartesian lines in dynamic projection would have become repetitive, perhaps obsessive, until it invaded the field of megastructures. In 1925 the Viennese Kiesler, another member of De Stijl, constructed a pavilion in the Expo des Arts Décoratifs in Paris, which was based on a similar concept to that of the structure designed by Rietveld in his theory of the city of the future: "A system of tensions within a free space. Change of space into urbanism. No foundation, no walls. Distance from the ground, suppression of the static axis. Creation of new possibilities for living, creation of a new society."[4]

Rietveld the man and his psychology are simple. Although he participated in avant-garde movements, he was never a propagandist but, rather, a patient builder who left it to others to formulate dogma. He certainly did not possess the dialectical ability, coherence of thought, or verbal synthesis of Van Doesburg nor even the theoretical organization of Mondrian, but like Oud and Mies van der Rohe he was a poet, and in architecture this means that he knew how to transmute materials and aims into works of arts. His intuition and direct approach were extraordinary and he succeeded in making his objects the connecting link between the abstraction of the painters of the group and the architectural utopia of the others. Together with the sculptures of Vantongerloo, the chairs of Rietveld inspired Van Doesburg and Van Eesteren in their theories of architecture. From chair to building, all his constructions are to be considered structuralist, just as the style in which they are conceived is structuralist. If the neoplasticism of De Stijl had never existed, Rietveld's work would be classified as structuralist only.[5] Unlike many other architects of his generation who thought of architecture as a cubic box, Rietveld employed the method of starting his constructions from the interior and working outward, as if to exemplify a Freudian complex. He thought of the construction as a "cage"—a cage which was not oppressive, which allowed space and light to filter through it, a structure like a system, where one could live, move, intervene, modify, or delimit the space. An essential cage, it was viewed as a mechanism made ready for the self-designing of the living area.

[1] For a detailed study of the semiological interpretation of communication, see Umberto Eco, *La struttura assente*,3rd ed.(Milan, 1968), especially "Architettura e comunicazione." See also the basic work by C. Morris, *Segni, linguaggio e comportamento*, Italian ed. (Milan, 1940).

[2] Theo van Doesburg, in *De Stijl*, II,11 (September 1919).

[3] Siegfried Giedion, *Mechanization Takes Command* (New York, 1948).

[4] Friederich Kiesler, *L'architecture élémentarisée*, in *De Stijl* (1927).

[5] Not "elementarist" as it is defined by Reyner Banham, *Theory and Design in the First Machine Age* (London, 1960), a limitative term not to be confused with the elementarist theory formulated by Van Doesburg in 1924 to explain the dynamics of the sloping plane.

The Early Years

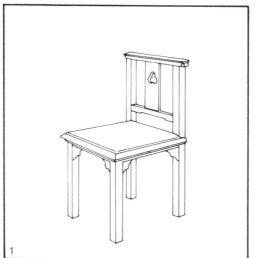

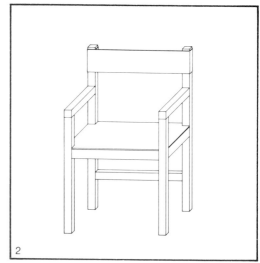

1. Zuilen stoel, 1900.
2. Leunstoel, 1908.
3. Stoel, 1915, executed after a design by P. J. Klaarhamer.
4. Stoel, 1915, executed after a design by P. J. Klaarhamer.
5. Buffet, 1915, executed after a design by P. J. Klaarhamer.
6. Kraalschroten kast, 1908-15.

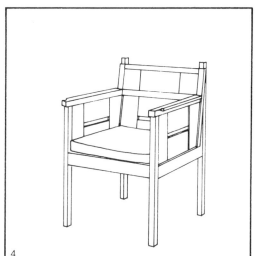

3

4

5

H. P. Berlage, sketches of shapes to be used in the construction of a sideboard, 1906.

E. W. Godwin, sideboard, 1867.

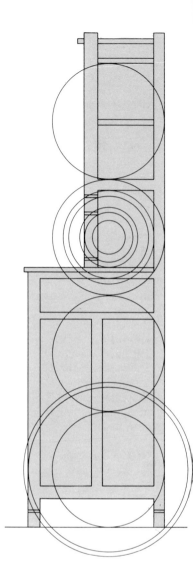

32

In his artistic evolution Rietveld always evinced a special and quite unusual quality: at every moment of his career he was an innovator. In everything with which he occupied himself there was always an idea, small or large, which led to experimentation and opened the way to new solutions, whether technological, material, or formal. From the age of twelve when he worked in his father's furniture workshop and executed stylistic imitations until he reached the stage of envisaging the sculpture pavilion at Sonsbeek, Arnhem (1954), with its space suggested but not defined and delimited only by a curtain of hot air, Rietveld has always worked with an eye to the future without ever letting himself be influenced by indigenous or historical restoration, but working with a clear and simple method and remaining imperturbable in the face of all that surrounded him, as if he had been given the task of replanning the world and as if before that time no chair had ever been constructed.[1]

C. R. Mackintosh, armchair, 1900.

There is little of particular interest in his personal life and, until the end of the Second World War at least, he pursued his profession quietly as did many others. We are told that he was born in Utrecht in 1888, where he lived practically his whole life, apart from occasional periods of travel or holidays abroad, in Europe, and (in the last years of his life) America. He left school after completing the elementary stage and became apprenticed to his father who was a cabinetmaker (1899); he later worked as a designer for the jeweller Cornelius J. Begeer (1906–11) and studied design at evening classes (1906–08). From 1908 to 1911 he followed a course in architectural design with P. Houtzagers; after 1911 he became an independent cabinetmaker and opened his own combined workshop and store at 93 Adriaan van Ostadelaan, Utrecht, while he attended an advanced course in architecture conducted by P.J. Klaarhamer (1911-15), a good architect working in association with Berlage. He later joined his studio. Klaarhamer was an important figure in Dutch architecture of that period and his workshop was entrusted with large-scale commissions in the fields of building, exhibition construction, and furnishing.

Rietveld's designs before the famous "Rood Blauwe" are small in number and do not reveal any particular influences or passions. The chair constructed in 1908, now in the Centraal Museum, Utrecht, was made of oak and leather and is the first notable object in his career as a designer. It certainly derived from Berlage, as did his design for a cupboard in 1911, but this cannot be considered at all remarkable because the great prestige of Berlage, his exceptional intellectual power and breadth of vision, had for many years acted as a catalyst for the whole generation which followed his own.

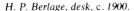

H. P. Berlage, desk, c. 1900.

The Dutch Nieuwe Kunst[2]
However, in order to arrive at a better understanding of this historical period we must examine its development more closely. While the Dutch art nouveau (Nieuwe Kunst) was inspired by the English Arts and Crafts movement and enjoyed continuous cultural exchanges with it, its mode of expression was simpler and more severe than the latter. It differed greatly from the form which developed in Belgium or in France but showed some affinity with the German style of the time. This produced at least three fundamental characteristics for the future development of art and architecture: (1) While keeping away from historicism, the deeply rooted Dutch medievalism was not abandoned and could be found right up to the time of the last exponents of the School of Amsterdam. (2) Into this background a Far Eastern element was incorporated. Interest in the Javanese art of batik invested all aspects of decoration. In most cases it took the form of two-dimensional decorative elements which adopted fantastic and organic shapes representing in silhouette form birds and insects together with geometrical ornamentation. This kind of decoration

33

G. Rietveld, sketch for a cupboard, 1911.

was adopted in textiles, in all graphic expressions, in personal objects and decor, and in architectural decoration itself. But in architecture it fulfilled a secondary function, limited to small friezes or as end pieces to terminal sections. (3) Its autonomous and local development generated the genius of Berlage.

As early as 1890 Berlage had accused the dominant architecture of Europe of deceit: "Our parents and grandparents as well as ourselves, have lived and still live in surroundings more hideous than any known before." Deceit is the rule—truth is the exception.[3] The Amsterdam Stock Exchange was his masterpiece (1898-1903) and served to achieve the purification of European architecture, becoming at the same time an example and stimulus to creation for a whole generation of young architects. Here the flat surface of the wall became the starting point for new architectural principles. Berlage declared: "In particular we must show the bare wall with all its naked beauty. . . . Pillars and columns should not have protruding capitals: the joints should be fused with the plane surface of the wall."[4]

Berlage himself as well as the Nieuwe Kunst—so modest a manifestation in comparison with art nouveau—were to have a great impact on the development of Dutch architecture and its influence on the architecture of Europe.

In the field of decor, the Netherlands has always employed a petit bourgeois artisan style which does not merit particular critical interest. The phenomenon of the spread of the Arts and Crafts movement throughout continental Europe represented for Rietveld a remote and negligible factor at the time when he was engaged on his first designs. After all, he had been made aware of the movement in a form filtered through with new connotations by Berlage. Berlage's furniture is quite simple and unadorned and is made of natural wood; it is influenced in its turn by Vosey and Ashbee to some extent, but by Mackmurdo and Godwin also from some points of view. At all events, the Netherlands was undergoing quite an intense period of activity in the field of decor and a gallery was opened in Amsterdam in 1900 devoted to interior decoration and household objects: "t'Binnenhuis Inrichting tot Meubilering en Versiering der Woning." This gallery was clearly inspired by the same principles which governed Arts and Crafts and attracted many of the artists of the time, from Berlage to Dijsselhof and Van den Bosch. Something else which may have interested Rietveld was the echo of the success being obtained everywhere in Europe by the Scottish designer Charles Rennie Mackintosh, another master of the Modern movement. Almost at the same date that Berlage constructed the Amsterdam Stock Exchange, Mackintosh erected a building which made him famous: the Glasgow School of Art. Together with his wife and sister-in-law, the Macdonald sisters, and his brother-in-law, Herbert McNair, also an architect, Mackintosh founded an artistic movement later known by the name of the Glasgow Style.

It seems that the vehicle for the exchange of information between Glasgow and the Netherlands was the English journal *Studio*, and it is by no means impossible that the famous painting by the best-known Dutch painter Jan Toorop, *De Drie Bruiden*, published in this journal[5] in 1893, could have influenced the decorative style of Mackintosh and other artists belonging to the School of Ghosts,[6] who were beginning to develop a similar style during those years. On the other hand, the same journal devoted a whole number to the Glasgow Style in 1900, thus making known the work of Mackintosh.

In the same year Mackintosh and his group took part in the Vienna International Exhibition, where they aroused great critical and public acclaim. Mackintosh was a great interior designer and a very sensitive creator of furniture: he could pass with ease from the elegant and flexible sphere of soft tonal harmonies to a rigidly geometrical form, employing a skillful interplay of heavy cubes, sharp corners, and rectilinear surfaces.

"What characterizes all Mackintosh furniture can be said to be a successful synthesis of the contrasting criteria of England and the Continent. . . . The hard verticals and horizontals must have been an attraction to Mackintosh in themselves, an aesthetic counterpoint to his tense curves, and a safeguard that the frail blooms and feminine hues do not cloy."[7]

An interesting comparison has been made between Mackintosh's work and neoplasticism: "Imbued with sublime poetry of line, the view of Mackintosh's work as a prophecy of neoplasticism must be stated with caution, since it applies only at a virtual and allusive level. He invents the breaking up of volumes into planes, and immediately turns to something else: he sings and does not try to establish a theoretical doctrine."[8]

It is easy to imagine that it was the more structural and functional part of Mackintosh's work which had a special appeal for Rietveld. Among the chairs designed by the great Scotsman he could not have failed to be more attracted by the less cerebral and more angular shapes, and less by the sensual and two-dimensionally graphic lines.

It is probable too that Rietveld was brought closer to Mackintosh by the book *Englische Haus* by Muthesius, published in Germany in 1904–05, where some examples of Mackintosh's furniture were shown. This book was well known in the Netherlands and esteemed by Berlage, De Klerk, and many other architects belonging to the School of Amsterdam. But apart from the important cultural influences which Rietveld met in his formative years, until at least the end of 1916, he made little advance on the oak and leather chair of 1908. We see this if we look at the furniture he designed for Klaarhamer in 1915: a chair, a dining-room chair, and a sideboard (all now in the Centraal Museum, Utrecht), which all derived from the teaching of Berlage, as did the 1908 chair. However, his formation was meditative, far-seeing, and adapted to the formulation of a primary language which, when used, made itself clear and unequivocal.

Above: *R. van't Hoff, study in plastic forms, 1918, published in* De Stijl, *no. 6, 1918; above bottom: detail of a bed executed in 1918.*

[1]Siegfried Giedion, *Space, Time, and Architecture*.
[2]For an exhaustive study of the art of this period, see Robert Schmutzler, *Art nouveau* (Stuttgart, 1962); S. Tschudi Madsen, *Art Nouveau* (London, 1967); Giovanni Fanelli, *Architettura moderna in Olanda*.
[3]Quoted in Siegfried Giedion, *Space, Time, and Architecture*. For the influence of Berlage on modern architecture, see also Bruno Zevi, *Poetica dell'architettura neoplastica* (Milan, 1953) and *Storia dell'architettura moderna* (Turin, 1950); Leonardo Benevolo, *Storia dell'architettura moderna* (Bari, 1966); Giovanni Fanelli, op. cit.

[4]H. Petrus Berlage, *Gedanken über den Stil in der Baukunst* (Leipzig, 1905).
[5]W. Shaw Sparrow, "Herr Toorop's, *The Three Bridges*," in *The Studio* (1893).
[6]The name many people gave to the Glasgow School of Art.
[7]Nikolaus Pevsner, *The Sources of Modern Architecture and Design* (New York, 1968). For a critical study of the furniture, see Filippo Alison, *Le sedie di Charles Rennie Mackintosh* (Casabella: Milan, 1973).
[8]Bruno Zevi, *Poetica dell'architettura neoplastica* (Milan, 1953).

1. LEUNSTOEL (Chair), 1908
Structure of natural oak; seat and chair back of brown leather; 55×40×86 cm.

Exh: Utrecht, 1958.

Repr.:   Les sources du XXe siècle, 1960-61; Cat. G. Rietveld architect, *1971.*

Coll.:   Utrecht, Centraal Museum.

Design and execution by Rietveld.

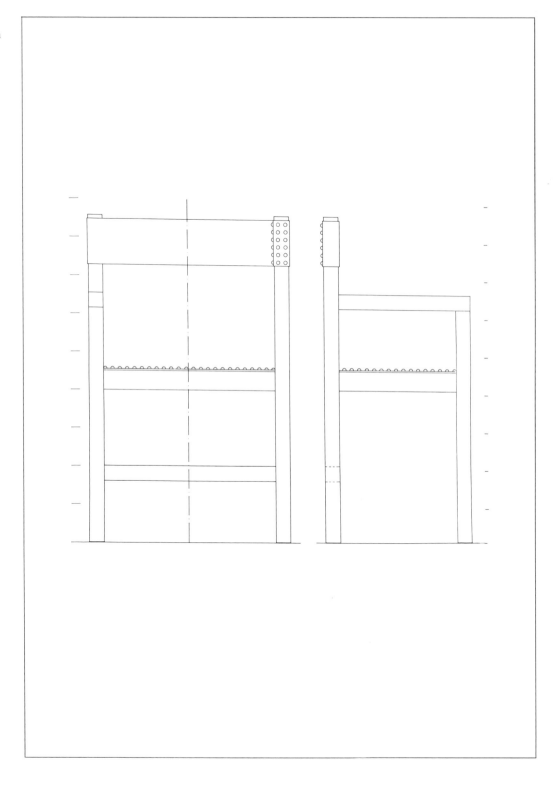

7

8

9

13

14

15

A Repetitive Structural Node:
38 **The Reinvented Object**

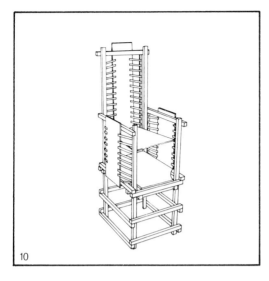

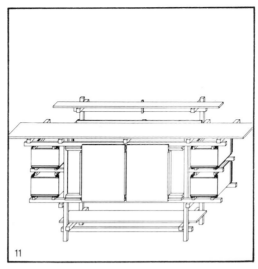

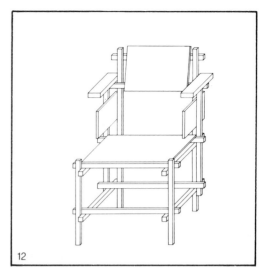

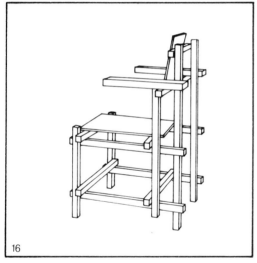

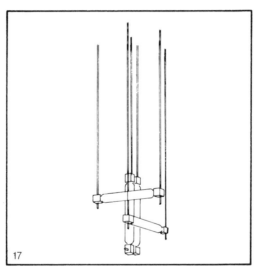

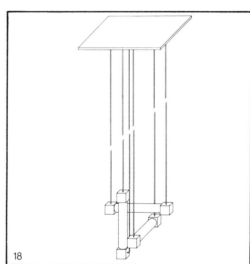

7. *Eerste model Rood Blauwe stoel*, c. 1917, *first
unpainted model.*
8. *Rood Blauwe stoel*, 1918.
9. *Bolderwagen*, 1918.
10. *Kinderstoel*, 1919.
11. *Beukenhouten dressoirtje*, 1919.
12. *Hoge stoel*, 1919.
13. *Stoel, tafel*, 1919, *furniture made for a house
belonging to Van Doesburg.*
14. *Kinderstoel*, 1919.
15. *Schelling-meubelen*, c. 1920.
16. *Maarssen-stoel*, 1920.
17. *Hanglamp*, 1920.
18. *Hanglamp, later version.*

Rietveld's drawing of the Cartesian node and the model now in the Centraal Museum, Utrecht.

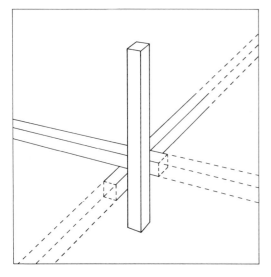

From the year 1916 onward Rietveld in his workshop in Adriaan van Ostadelaan, Utrecht, experimented in entirely new ways of building, which led him to find a structural node formed of three listels with quadrangular section which he superimposed on juxtaposed connections, placed perpendicular to each other, according to the Cartesian coordinates: abscissa, ordinate, and zenith. This method enabled him to discover the possibility of employing a repetitive method which was practically unlimited if applied to the creation of furniture.

The basic concept was provided by those elements which could be made to continue the length of their axes, in a kind of mechanism whose pivot was formed by the sliding nodes: at the instant when the elements take up the desired position and are identified in the required object (with the addition of some extra planes) the figure becomes crystallized. At this point Rietveld decided to construct a chair, applying to its dimensions and proportions the rules he had previously learned when he was working in Klaarhamer's studio. This structural node and this large chair were to have a determining influence in the future, not only regarding his own activity and work, but also, and mainly, in helping some of the painters of the time to arrive at a satisfactory definition of the neoplastic style, which at that time was in process of formation.

It was in 1918, after he had become a member of the group which centered around the journal *De Stijl*, born the year before, that he simplified the large chair by removing some of its superstructure and slightly reducing its size. Then, the primary colors advocated by Bart van der Leck, who shared Klaarhamer's studio at the time, were applied to the chair which then became known by its present title "Rood Blauwe" (more usually given the English name "Red and Blue").

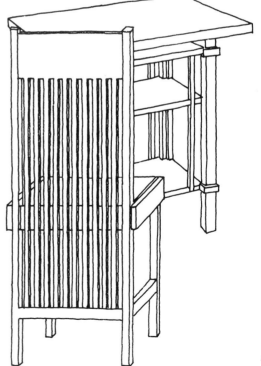

F. L. Wright, furniture for Coonly House, Riverside, 1908.

Of the members of the De Stijl group, Rietveld had for several years been a friend of Robert van't Hoff, who on his return from a visit to the United States, from 1914 to 1916, built two important reinforced concrete constructions at Huis ter Heide near Utrecht. These provided the first indications of the architectural (and technological) revival in the Netherlands, and alongside the design by Oud for workers' homes of 1917, and Wils' inn at Woerden, again of 1917, they constitute the first stage of De Stijl architecture. In the Huis ter Heide, Van't Hoff expressed all that he had learned from Frank Lloyd Wright, whom he had met in Chicago; in particular, he was influenced by Cheney House, Oak Park (1904), and Robie House, Chicago (1908).[1] In this way Rietveld discovered the work of the American architect at second hand, through his friend Van't Hoff, and was impressed also by the rigid chairs designed by Wright from 1904 onward. These images made such a strong impression on his mind that they formed the predominant feature of his background and one of the very few cultural influences in his life.

The collaboration between Van't Hoff and Rietveld in those years was very productive; the former asked his friend to construct the furniture which he himself designed, so contributing to the close affinities of taste between the two men. Van't Hoff also asked Rietveld to design the interior of the 1916 house "in the manner of Wright," but no trace of this project remains; the furniture has been dispersed and no photographs survive to testify to its value. This was the time when Rietveld was working on the structural system of the future "Rood Blauwe" and the other early furniture based on the same principle of construction.

The "Rood Blauwe"
With its particular structural origin, the "Rood Blauwe" must be considered a special case. In fact, in the whole of Europe we can find no indications which lead to its direct influence. With regard to Wright, although Rietveld came under his spell in a general

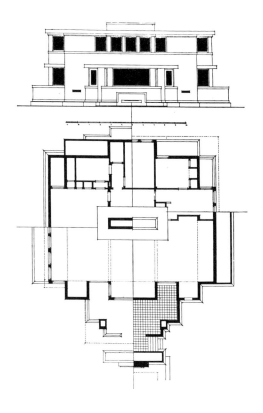

R. van 't Hoff, house built of reinforced concrete at Huis ter Heide, 1916: view over the garden and plans of the two levels (above), detail of the veranda (below).

sense, the idea for this node with tangential and self-supporting listels developing dynamic structures did not belong to the method employed by the great American architect.

To single out a previously existing type of construction to which this structural node could be related one could refer to a technique of American origin: the "Ballon frame."[2] This is a method of employing thin planks used in carpentry for the building of inexpensive homes, but it is highly unlikely that Rietveld was aware of its existence.

It is usual for the relationship of an object to history to be perceived against the background of other objects and in association with them, in other words, as modifications of precise constant factors. Such a historical relationship is almost nonexistent in the case of the "Rood Blauwe."

As has been said, the chair is made up of a series of listels with quadrangular section, crisscrossing each other vertically and horizontally to imprint a reciprocal dynamism and concluding in a carrying structure. Two planes which rest very lightly and do not touch each other act as the seat and the back.

In the first unpainted version, two planes had been placed at the sides along the axis of the arms; these were later eliminated and represented the last typical element of the traditional "closed in" armchair. The various parts were so assembled that each could exist autonomously, in an unusual spatial harmony; but they were also intersected and extended in all directions, without ever ending in a groove. Lines and planes were organized in a vertical-horizontal composition, in which the space was not enclosed by the form, but filtered through it, so emphasizing the dynamic force which developed outward from the interior.

The first version of the chair was designed by Rietveld on a grill pattern with a basic unit of 10 cm. and the structural listel measuring a third of this unit, or 3.3 cm. The geometrical mechanism which emerged was simple and elementary and by this criterion could be constructed without the use of any working drawings. The width of the seat, for example, was indicated in four units, or 40 cm.; the back, three and one-third units, or 33 cm.; the side, six units in all. As we have seen, in 1918 Rietveld made some modifications to the chair and reduced the thickness of the listels to 2.5 x 2.6 cm. The whole chair was thus reduced proportionally.

The term "seat" is here used in a generic sense: it must be stated that its iconographic value does not permit of an easy classification. It is neither a true chair nor an armchair, at least as this is understood in western civilization. One might speak of a large chair suited to conversation, similar to some rigid but comfortable chairs found in Puritan New England.

Concerning its primary function one can say that when the body is in the correct position, the chair is certainly comfortable in spite of its rigidity.[3] All the parts seem prepared to welcome and transmit again the dynamic tension received by the body, the seat and the back, down to the horizontal bars and up again to the supporting verticals. Rietveld himself wrote of the "Rood Blauwe" in 1919: "In this seat an attempt has been made to keep each part absolutely simple in its form, and more elementary in line with its function and the material employed, a form, therefore, more able to harmonize with the whole. The construction of the various parts must be accorded in such a way that no single one of them predominates or is subordinated to the others. In this way the whole article is arranged freely and clearly in space and the form is borne directly from the material, predominating over it. This wooden structure makes it possible to construct a large chair with listels of 2.5 x 2.6 cm."[4]

When he came to apply color, Rietveld interpreted the neoplastic pictorial theory, lucidly apprehended by Mondrian, of neutralizing the form so as to cancel out any natural aspect, and in this way he followed a process of dematerialization, placing emphasis on the vertical-horizontal relationship of the straight lines, in an asymmetrical composition acting as a framework to the red and blue rectangles. Referring to neutrality of form, Mondrian wrote: "The more neutral the plastic means are, the more one can determine the immutable expression of reality. We can consider as relatively neutral those forms which show no relationship with the natural appearance of things or with any kind of idea."[5]

With the "Rood Blauwe" Rietveld obtained an abstract-concrete composition which was perfectly neoplastic and in line with the work of the De Stijl painters.

The first critical judgment on the chair was made in 1920 by Van Doesburg. In a futuristic type of literary text he showed its relationship to the metaphysical work of De Chirico and arrived at this type of definition:

> Contrast and similarity;
> > Contrast in significance, in expression, in method;
> > Similarity in metaphysical sensibility and mathematical indication of spaces.
> In both: spaces surrounded by spaces;
> > Individualization of spaces; mystique of spaces.

And further on, describing Rietveld's chair:

> A relationship of open spaces with an element of contrast:
> > FUNCTION TO SIT—CHAIR
> Material limitation against unlimited and clear image fixed to open spaces:
> > CHAIR
> Mute eloquence like a machine.[6]

Much later, in 1963, in an interview filmed by Piet van Monk, Rietveld spoke with the simplicity which always distinguished him about his chair and took from it the metaphysical aura imprinted on it by Van Doesburg: "The so-called 'Rood Blauwe,' the chair composed of two laths and a series of listels, was created with the intention of demonstrating that an aesthetic and spatial object could be constructed with linear material and made by machinery. I therefore sectioned the central part of the plank into two, obtaining a seat and a back; then, with listels of varying lengths, I constructed the chair. When I made it I did not realize that it would have such an enormous significance for me and also for others, nor did I imagine that its effect would be so overwhelming even in architecture. When the opportunity arose for me to build a house based on the same principles, I naturally did not let it pass me by."[7] Here he was obviously referring to the Schröder Huis.

This description seems too simplistic in view of the scale of his achievement and merits additional consideration. As Ragghianti wrote: "The primitivism or primary quality of Rietveld, however, is illusory, his simplicity, or more precisely his simplification, are the result of a prolonged and most careful calculation, a conscious selection, and not an instinctive matter at all. A close examination of Rietveld's scholarship, a deeply researched, conscious, and carefully thought out approach when compared with what went before or after him, shows that even at the start of his career the artist possessed a mature refinement, a subtlety of thought in no way untried but supported by a formal intelligence which carried forward to an artistic spontaneity a result containing no element of immediacy, or urgency, or abandonment and fluency. 'The invention' is not abrupt, and the conclusion presents a harmonious and perfectly balanced vision at every point, and especially at the points where an asymmetrical rhythm is in force or there are interrelationships among formal elements brought close together and set at a distance."[8]

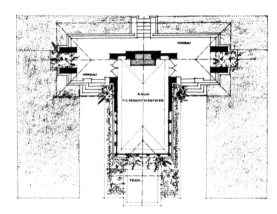

F. L. Wright, "Petit Memorial Chapel," Belvedere III: ground plan and side view.

43

Linear composition in the Rood Blauwe: below: structural plan of the side; on the right: dynamic-spatial projection of the lines through the structural node; below: method of assembly.

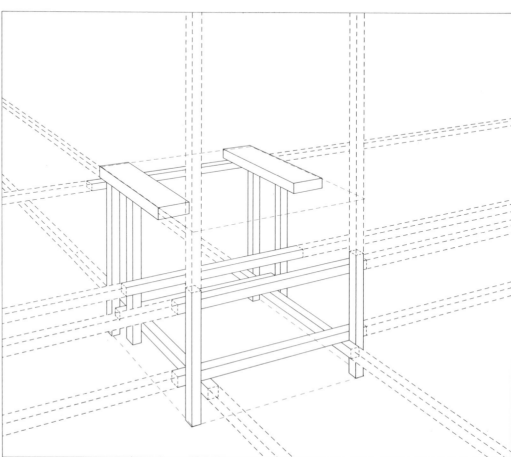

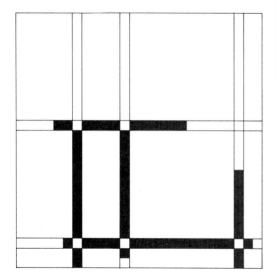

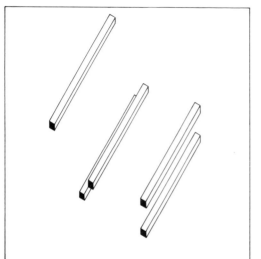

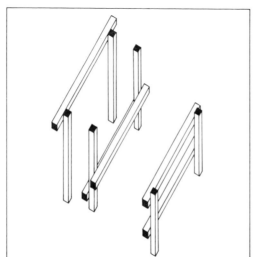

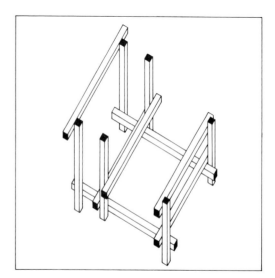

The theory according to which Rietveld constructed the "Rood Blauwe" and the other furniture inspired by the same principle is, as we have seen, so simple and elementary that it permits of a construction of the various parts by planes, according to the most rational industrial logic. In fact, when Rietveld designed his furniture he thought of the possibility of manufacturing it by repetitive mechanical means and making it available at a very moderate cost. He hoped at the same time—in line with a romantic view of society—to be able to free the artisan from the fatigue of manual labor. He associated the concept of industrialization with the ideal of progress, as in fact from Muthesius onward did all those who adhered to the historical avant-garde movements of the first two decades of this century, without of course being able to foresee the disadvantages which, with the growth of modern capitalism, were often to follow in the wake of industrialization.

"Craftsmanship is attached to an individualistic system of life, whereas the machine represents a decisive element in our economic and collectivist style. Craftsmanship humiliates man by reducing him to the function of a machine, while the right use of the machine represents the only way of achieving the contrary effect: social emancipation."[9] This idea of Van Doesburg's reflected the tendency followed by all the artists of his time, including Gropius and Le Corbusier,[10] who frequently extolled the machine. In any event it can be affirmed that Rietveld's view of industrial production was based on a perfect balance between the "human" values of craftsmanship and mass production, where, however, man was to remain the intelligent artifact who was to coordinate all phases of the operation carried out by machinery.

The Sideboard of 1919
Of all the furniture created by Rietveld, this sideboard relates most directly to an historical origin: its Japanese element derives from precise memories acquired during his early years as well as in all probability from the influence which Wright had upon him. The idea Rietveld conceived of how best to design an article of furniture for use as a sideboard was based on his most obvious cultural influences: the example of Berlage and the Anglo-Saxon tradition. The sideboard may be said to have originated directly in experiments both inside and outside the English Arts and Crafts movement.

The large sideboard made about the year 1877 by Edward William Godwin cannot have been unknown to Rietveld. Godwin was the greatest exponent of English aestheticism. He invented what he described as the Anglo-Japanese style which was, in effect, a highly personal style that he adopted when he furnished his own house in Bristol (1862), the White House of James McNeill Whistler in Chelsea (1877-78), and the house of Oscar Wilde in Tite Street, London (1884).

The quadrangular section which was the basis of Godwin's structure, in its spatial dynamics with the purity of line of a cage,[11] can be directly related to Rietveld's sideboard.

But if the origin of Rietveld's sideboard is to be sought in new and early rationalism, it is immediately apparent that his intentions were far removed from any kind of aesthetic inquiry. The basic premise from which he departed was, in this case too, the de-composition and disintegration of volume, which was cubist in origin and an essential part of the neoplastic doctrine, followed by its reconstitution into dynamic and spatial elements. Writing of this sideboard, Bruno Zevi said: "In opening the doors of a cupboard by Rietveld one experiences an extraordinary pleasure which derives not only from its technical perfection, but from the natural process of retracing the history of its assembly, which can be discovered and brought to life again, element by element, with amazing clarity."[12]

Rietveld used the skeleton of the furniture, that is, its structural node, as if it were part of an exciting game, into which he then inserted flat planes, shelving, and drawers. The horizontality of the planes was counterbalanced by the vertical ribbing whose task was to keep suspended the central body which served as container, while at the same time giving emphasis to the spatial dynamics. This characteristic was certainly not common to the usual two-dimensional fronts of similar articles of furniture. Although it was meant as a sideboard, its form is open and could even be enlarged into an almost infinitely repeated structure which would automatically place it in an entirely unforeseeable spatial relationship.

According to one of Lao-tse's maxims, a vessel is useful only on account of its emptiness. It must be said that just as in the case of Godwin's large sideboard, Rietveld's too was inferior in its function as a container to the effort of planning which created it. Once again the primary function, its *utilitas*, assumed a subordinate role. To use semantic terminology, it may be said that if we attribute the value of a signifying element to the structural form and that of the signified element to the container parts, then in this case the signifying element has replaced the primary function and tended to eliminate it.

Objects for Children

Also in 1918-19, Rietveld designed some playthings for children; this was probably due to family necessity or, perhaps, he wished to enjoy the pleasure of making toys for his own children. This activity permitted him to show his considerable gift for teaching, although he did not pursue this interest later unless we consider his work as a rationalist architect after 1924 to be pedagogical. The objects he made were: a baby buggy (plate 3), a cart, and two high chairs (photos on pages 13 and 45). In constructing the buggy he anticipated slightly the system of juxtaposed connections and relative integration between planes and structure which he completed in his design of the sideboard in 1919. In this case too, Rietveld started with a traditional object which he de-composed, sectioned, and reconstructed, assigning to each element an entirely new semantic significance. Still in the atmosphere of the "Rood Blauwe," he painted the buggy in the primary colors of yellow, red, blue, white, and black—which in any case are the most suitable colors for a simple learning toy.

A different color scheme was employed in the high chair on page 45 (Kinderstoel), which appeared for the first time in volume II of *De Stijl*.[13] The wooden framework was painted green; the straps which run along the structure were made of red leather with the hooks glazed bright green; a red leather cushion could also be placed against the back. The use of red together with its complementary color was quite unusual among the De Stijl artists who were unswervingly loyal to the primary colors. However, it is likely that the choice of these colors was due exclusively to the application of a personal psychological interpretation of color with the needs of a child in mind—if we consider the different visual perception produced from the interior of the seat, that is, from a close distance, and from its exterior, where the materials tend to amalgamate and fuse into a rhythmical and kinetic structure.

Rietveld himself described the chair in *De Stijl*: "Starting from the obvious requirements which emerge in designing this kind of object, such as making the chair comfortable to sit on and sturdy, adjustable in height, easy to clean, strong without being unduly heavy, I have aimed at the structural regularity of the object itself. . . . The front part which acts as a gate and the upper ledge are removable. . . . It takes only a short time to make, and this is in line with modern systems of production. There is the possibility moreover of using the module freely, which is thus expressed spatially insofar as it is freed from the plane of construction."[14] In fact, the visual impact of this chair is quite impressive: its primordial appearance could have been imagined by early man for some strange kind of tribal ceremony.

Apart from its skeletal supporting structure, which was common to all his chairs of this period, here Rietveld has added the leather straps which help to enclose the four sides as in a cage, enriching his style which until then had been bare and severe.

The other high chair, also produced in 1919, is more closely related to the "Hoge stoel," also of the same period.

The "Hoge Stoel" (Highback Chair), 1919

This chair, too, whose size we should perhaps today consider rather cumbersome, belongs to the same creative period as the "Rood Blauwe." As before, in the first version of the latter, Rietveld retained the two side pieces and did not paint the surface. Only the terminal sections of the structure and arms were painted, almost as if to signify an interruption in the composition. This chair appeared for the first time in volume III of *De Stijl*[15] beside the photograph of the sideboard. In the same year Van Doesburg presented an experimental decor with furniture by Rietveld.[16] This consisted of the "Hoge stoel," together with another version of it for use as a dining chair, and a table. It was already apparent that the De Stijl idea was moving away from the two-dimensional plane of the picture to the encompassing of space in a totally neoplastic environment. When Rietveld was invited in 1923 to participate in a Bauhaus exhibition, he sent this chair to Weimar; other Dutch exhibitors who were members of the group included Oud and Wils. But it was Rietveld's participation which aroused the immediate interest of Van Doesburg who, together with Van Eesteren and the collaboration of Rietveld himself, was working in that year on his design for the house of Léonce Rosenberg in Paris.[17]

In 1920 Rietveld introduced the "Hoge stoel" into his furniture for Dr. Hartog's study in Maarssen,[18] but this time the side pieces had been finally abandoned and the chair was painted all over. In this study at Maarssen there appeared also for the first time the hanging lamp made of neon tubes (Hanglamp). This lamp, which hangs freely in space in an asymmetrical perpendicular arrangement according to the Cartesian order, also repeats the pattern of the structural node which was common to all Rietveld's other furniture. The neon tubes are rectilinear segments, two vertical and two horizontal, crossing each other perpendicularly (later Rietveld was to eliminate one of the vertical segments, reducing the lamp to three elements only). The electrical wires are channelled into transparent tubes, descending from a square board affixed to the ceiling and attached to the two ends of each tube.

Having examined these early objects, we can observe how Rietveld brought about the total and absolute destruction of the traditional appearance of objects by means of his method of breaking up volumes and reconstituting them into new and simplified structures defined by a code of rules which was at once visual and structural. As a result of this method the object emerges not only renewed, but entirely reinvented, and the traditional methods of making furniture have been superseded. In the same way, neoplastic painting has annulled centuries of subjective art and made itself neutral and elemental to the ends of achieving a more universal equilibrium.

Toward a Formal Genesis

We have examined the historical context in which Rietveld's artistic development originated, noted the background out of which he emerged, analyzed the structural and idiomatic approach he adopted in constructing his first articles of furniture, especially the "Rood Blauwe," and discussed the functional values of the object. But in order to grasp

G. Rietveld, reconstruction of the jeweller's shop Goud en Zilversmids Co., Amsterdam, 1920-22.

all the intrinsic values of a semantic nature contained in the object and of a psychic nature for anyone in the position of observer, it is necessary to delve more deeply into certain concepts so as to arrive at an interpretation as little approximative and empirical as possible. The rhythmic and spatial dynamism expressed by Rietveld's furniture of this period and by all the works of the neoplastic movement can be explained today only by reference to the Gestalt theory, the theory which brought about a true visual revolution and came fully into being after the first decade of this century through the works of some German scholars, especially Wertheimer, Koffka, and Köhler. These men arrived at the dynamic theory of sensorial organization after a consideration of the various discoveries of the still young science of psychology which they criticized and challenged until they finally arrived at the formulation of "Gestaltism."

According to this theory, a straight line is not only the shortest distance between two points,[19] as believed by the ancient Greeks, but should be thought of as a point in movement toward another point. In the same way, a plane is to be thought of as a series of lines in movement, and a volume as planes in movement. Therefore the vitality of an equilibrium always depends upon the entity of the opposing forces which counterpose and balance each other; in our case, lines and planes, horizontals and verticals. When two lines cross, the fields of force struggle and the spatial energies are concentrated at the angle produced. And again, the open network of lines leads in various directions into space, so achieving a dynamic spatial construction.

This point reflects the key concept of Mondrian's view of space, where rectangles are spaces "where lines cross or touch each other tangentially, without for this reason ceasing to continue."[20]

It is clear that the De Stijl artists, especially Mondrian who more than the others established a rigorous theory of neoplasticism, had intuitively interpreted—though without being personally acquainted with them—the theoretical studies of problems of perception which were being undertaken during those years by philosophers and psychologists. [21]

Apart from the question of form and representation, the other aspect which is of particular interest for a comprehension of the period under review is that of color.

It is known that for Gestalt psychologists the centrifugal and centripetal forces of planes of contrasting colors move in tension in all directions, forcing the viewer to a kinetic participation, while following the intrinsic spatial direction of the colors. The dynamic quality is founded on the movement of plastic forces in their tendency to reach equilibrium.

The structural use of color can provide a sensation of spatial reality never arrived at by any other methods of representation. As we have seen, the De Stijl artists—including Rietveld in his early furniture—held rigidly to the principle of primary colors—red, blue and yellow—together with the use of noncolors like gray, white, and black, and rejected the contamination of complementary and secondary colors.

[1] In the first volume of Wasmuth's monograph on the work of Wright published in Germany in 1910 and later made known all over Europe, the Robie House did not yet appear.

[2] G. E. Woodward, *Country Homes* (Chicago, 1869). Quoted in Siegfried Giedion, *Space, Time and Architecture*.

[3] Much has been said concerning the rigidity of this chair, as if comfort were the only requirement of its occupant, the *utilitas primaria*. In fact, to provide a place to sit is but one of its functions, the most immediate but perhaps not the most important. From this viewpoint we must consider the idea of "function" in a wider context to include all the messages communicated by the object, not least of which are its semantic and symbolical connotations, which are no less useful than its strictly functional aspects. We refer here to a more general concept of the primary function of the object, expressed previously by Umberto Eco, *La struttura assente*.

[4] Quoted by Van Doesburg, in *De Stijl*, II, 11 (September 1919).

[5] Piet Mondrian, *Essays*.

[6] Theo van Doesburg, in *De Stijl*, III, 5 (March 1920).

[7] From the catalogue to the retrospective exhibition of Rietveld held at the Stedelijk Museum, Amsterdam, in November 1971.

[8] Carlo Ragghianti, in *Selearte*, 50 (1961), a review of T. M. Brown, *The Work of G. Rietveld, Architect*.

[9] Theo van Doesburg, quoted in Bruno Zevi, *Poetica dell' architettura neoplastica*.

[10] At least two different views of the place of the "machine" in art emerged among the adherents of the historical avant-garde movements: the first was of a positivist type expressed by the Deutscher Werkbund, from Muthesius through the Bauhaus, believing in a reasonable and positive use of the machine; the other was more irrational and was expressed in violent terms by the futurists and some expressionists.

[11] Hugh Honour, *Cabinet Makers and Furniture Designers* (London, 1969).

[12] Bruno Zevi, *Poetica dell'architettura neoplastica*.

[13] Published in *De Stijl*, II, 9 (July 1919).

[14] Published in *De Stijl*, II, 9 (July 1919).

[15] Published in *De Stijl*, III, 5 (March 1920).

[16] Published in *De Stijl*, III, 12, (November 1920).

[17] As is known, Van Doesburg was a guest at Weimar from 1921 to the end of 1922 but was forced to leave because his quarrelsome nature and his dogmatism aroused hostility. Embittered by his friend's participation in this exhibition, he wrote to him from Paris: "This morning when I awoke I found a number of letters, and among the others there was one from Germany; enclosed was a program of the Bauhaus-Week. I was stunned to see in it that you had joined in the exposition of the Bauhaus in Weimar, thus working *against* De Stijl. That Wils and Oud joined does not surprise me very much; they are constantly advertising themselves. But what advantage can you see in exhibiting *there*. I feel very miserable and now realize that I must give up the De Stijl-idea because I am gradually, due to encircling intrigues, standing alone. This entire Bauhaus display results from the struggle which I had there; the exposition is intended as an immediate revenge against my influence and against my person. Gropius, the director, will use this demonstration only as a *raison d'être* for the Bauhaus and as a means of perpetuating it." (from Theodore M. Brown, op. cit.).

[18] Publisned in *De Stijl*, VI, 3-4 (May-June 1923).

[19] Archimedes, *Concerning the Sphere and Cylinder*.

[20] Piet Mondrian, *Le neoplasticisme*.

[21] The basic theory of Gestalt was interpreted and taken as the basis for experimentation during the 1920s—often in a personal manner—by others as well as Mondrian, including Malevich, Kandinsky, and Klee. It was not until about 1928, however, after the Bauhaus had moved to Berlin, that the theory began to circulate in cultural and artistic circles. But the theories of form and color viewed as movement and as the dynamics of perception, and extended not only to the pictorial field but also to the spatial field of architecture, did not become precisely formulated until around 1935, after the Nazis had gained control of Germany and many artists, critics, and scholars emigrated to the United States. Among those who have contributed to making the new conceptions widely known, obviously with different interpretations, yet all determining for the construction of a new manner of conceiving art and visual communication, mention must be made of George Kepes, Siegfried Giedion, and Lazlo Moholy-Nagy, as well as the previously mentioned Wolfgang Köhler and Kurt Koffka.

G. Rietveld, Dr. Hartog's clinic, Maarssen, 1920.

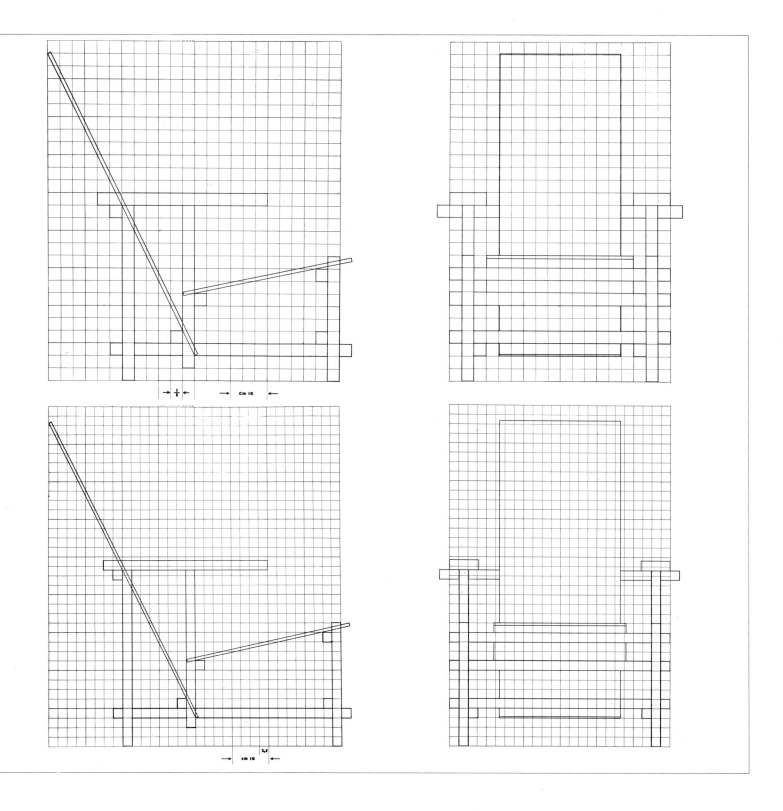

cm 10

cm 10   2,5

2. ROOD BLAUWE STOEL (Red and Blue), 1918. Built in deal with ebony aniline dye; back, seat, and terminals lacquered red, blue, and yellow; 60×84×86 cm. (in the final version).

Exh: Haarlem, 1919; New York, 1936; Amsterdam, 1951; New York, 1952; Venice, 1952; Utrecht, 1958; Amsterdam, 1971; London, 1972; Zürich, 1973.

Repr. T. van Doesburg, 1919; "Tentoonstelling Aesthetisch . . ." 1919; "Nederlandsche Ambachts . . ." 1920; *Mert*, 1923; J. Havelaar, 1924; *Binnenhuis*, 1928; A. G. Schneck, 1928; J. de Jong, 1929; *De 8 en Opbouw*, 1935; A. H. Barr, 1936; Cat. 81 *De Stijl*, 1951; B. Zevi, 1953; A. H. Barr, 1954; W. van der Pluym, 1954; H. L. C. Jaffé, 1956; W. Sandberg, 1957; T. M. Brown, 1958; H. Schaafsma, 1959; R. Banham, 1960; A. van Onck, 1965; G. Veronesi, 1967; G. Fanelli, 1968; H. Honour, 1969; P. Overy, 1969; C. Meadmore, 1974; B. Zevi, 1974.

Coll.: Amsterdam, Stedelijk Museum; The Hague Gemeentemuseum; New York, Museum of Modern Art.

A first unpainted version of the chair was made by Rietveld in 1917-18. It was made of oak, with larger dimensions than the present version and the quadrangular listel section measuring 3.3 cm.; there were two side panels in addition.
Rietveld arrived at his present version after he had become a member of De Stijl. The various replicas scattered in museums and private collections were all executed by G. van de Groenekan. Since 1971 the chair has been in regular production under international license by Cassina, Meda.

On the left: *the first unpainted version of the Rood Blauwe, published in* De Stijl, *no. 11, 1919;* below: *the elements which compose the armchair.*

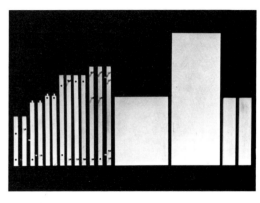

51

3. BOLDERWAGEN (Baby buggy), *c.* 1918.
Made out of deal lacquered white, black, red, blue,
and yellow; 65×125×60 cm.

Exh.:   Utrecht, 1958; London, 1968; Amsterdam,
1971.

Repr.:   *Vouloir*, 1927; T. M. Brown, 1958.

Coll.:   Amsterdam, Stedelijk Museum; Meda,
Cassina.

Design and execution by Rietveld.

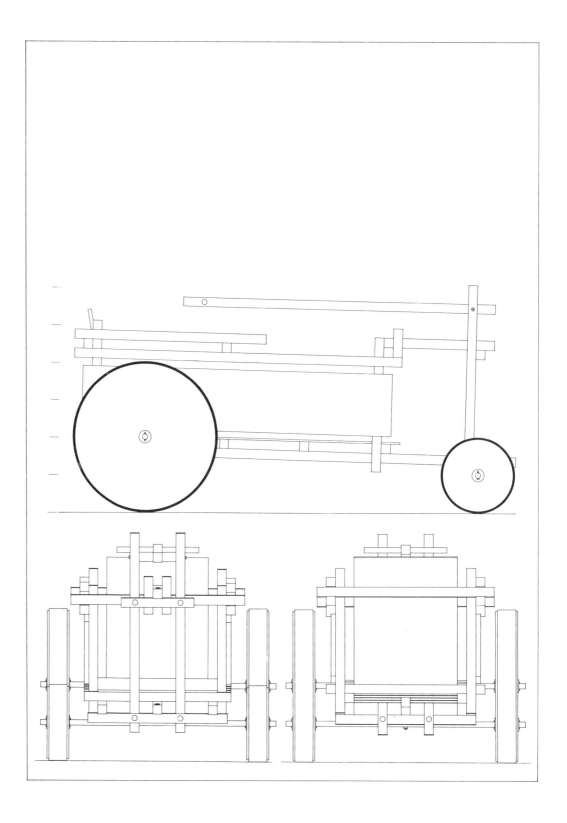

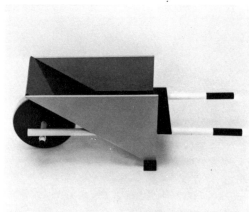

Below: *Kinderkruiwagen, 1920.*

4.   BEUKENHOUTEN DRESSOIRTJE (Buffet),
1919.
Deal with white aniline dye; 195×104×45 cm.

Exh.:   Amsterdam, 1951; New York, 1952; Venice,
1952; Utrecht, 1958; Rome, 1967; Amsterdam, 1971;
London, 1972.

Repr.:   T. van Doesburg, 1920; J. J. P. Oud, 1921; G.
Rietveld, 1927; S. Giedion, 1948; *Wonen*, 1956; H. L.
C. Jaffé, 1956; T. M. Brown, 1958; H. L. C. Jaffé,
1967; H. Honour, 1969; P. Overy, 1969.

Coll.:   Amsterdam, Stedelijk Museum (replica).

Design and execution by Rietveld.
The original was destroyed in a fire. It is believed to
have been constructed of natural oak.

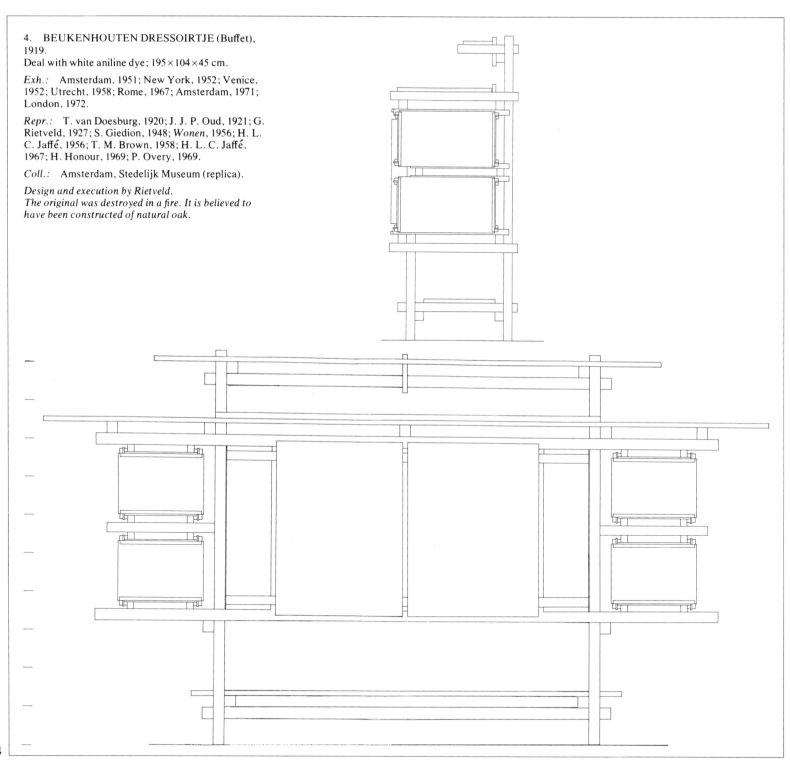

Above: *photo published in* De Stijl, *no. 5, 1920.*

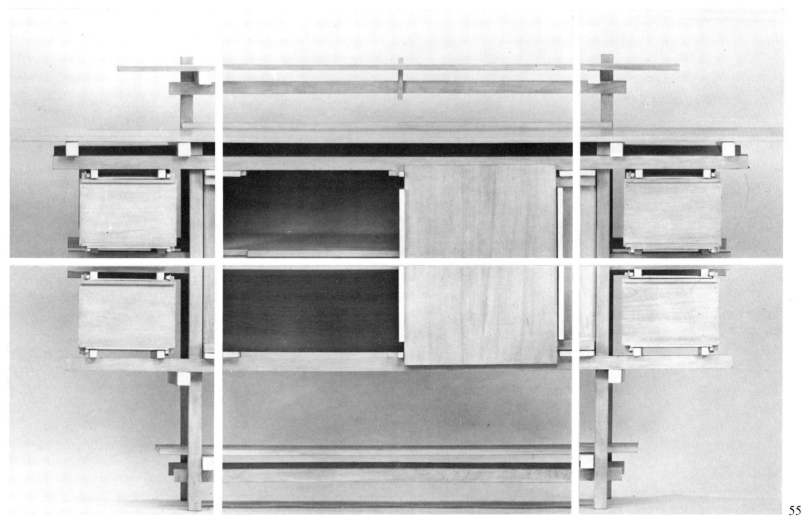

5. HOGE STOEL (Highback chair), 1919.
Structure of natural oak with terminals lacquered
violet; 60×60×93 cm.

Exh.: Weimar, 1923; Utrecht, 1958; Amsterdam,
1971; London, 1972.

Repr.: *De Stijl,* 1920; T. van Doesburg, 1920; *De
Stijl,* 1922; *L'architecture vivante,* 1925; W. Sandberg,
1957; T. M. Brown, 1958; P. Overy, 1969.

Coll.: Amsterdam, Stedelijk Museum (replica).

Design and execution by Rietveld.
This chair appeared for the first time in De Stijl, *no. 12,
1920, as part of a decor designed by Van Doesburg,
dated 1919. The same chair was later placed by
Rietveld in the clinic at Maarssen (1920), but without
the two original side panels.*

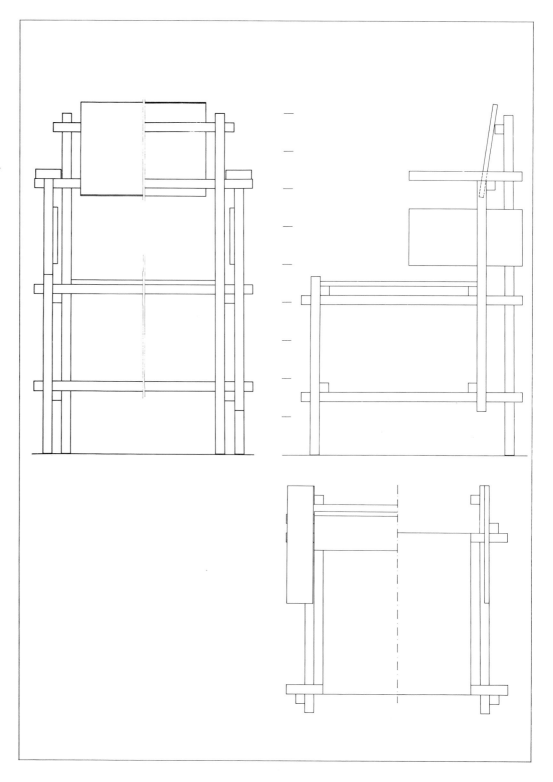

56

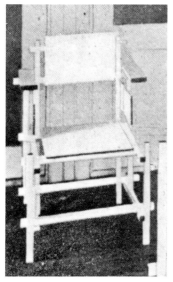

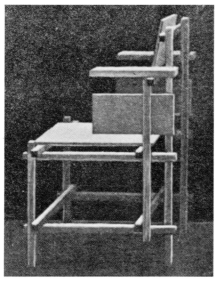

Left: *detail of the interior furnished by Doesburg in 1919 with furniture by Rietveld*; right: *the armchair as it was published in* De Stijl, *no. 5, 1920.*

6. HANGLAMP (Hanging lamp), 1920.
Neon tube lights, cubic terminals made of ebonized
oak; 35×35×130 cm. approx. (variable height).

Exh.: Utrecht, 1958; Amsterdam, 1959.

Repr.: De Stijl, 1923; *Bouwkundig Weekblad,* 1924;
B. Taut, 1924; El Lissitzky, 1926; J. J. P. Oud, 1926;
Wonen, 1956; T. M. Brown, 1958; *Architectural
Design,* 1965; P. Overy, 1969.

Coll.: Utrecht, G. van de Groenekan; Utrecht,
Schröder Huis.

*Design and execution by Rietveld for the Maarssen
clinic.*
*The lamp which was later placed in the Schröder Huis
is a variant of the first design and consists of only three
tubes instead of four.*

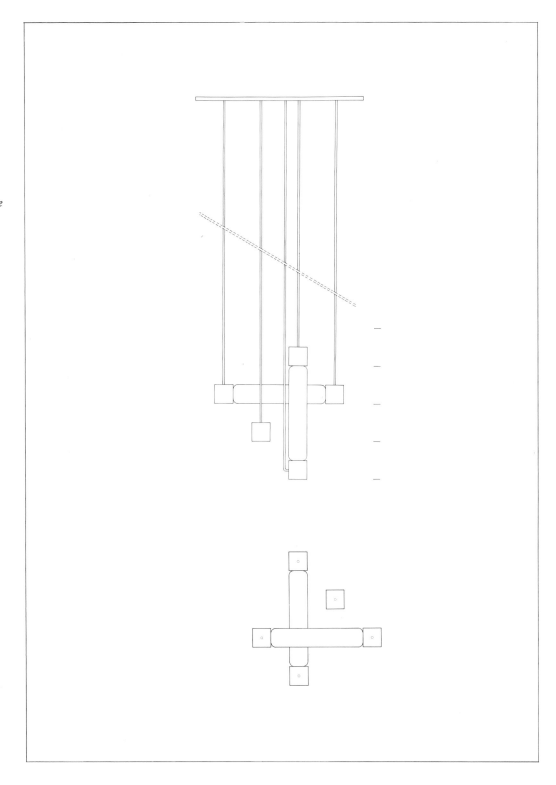

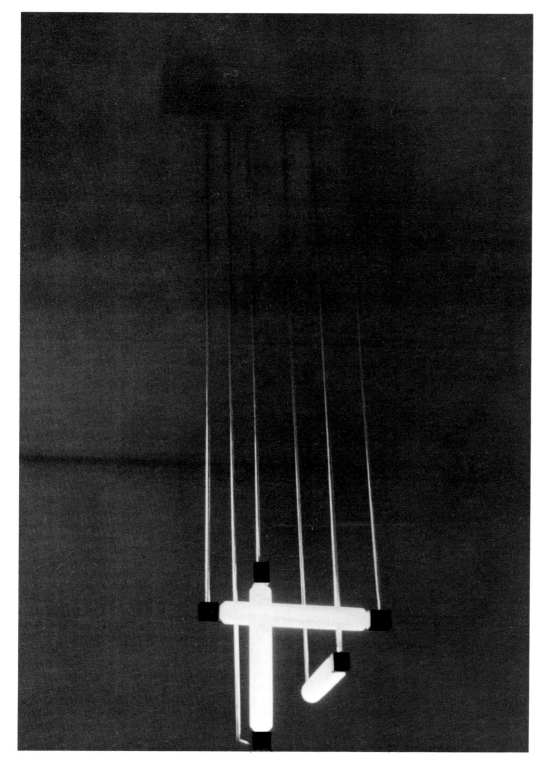

The lamp designed for *Dr. Hartog's* clinic at Maarssen.

Related Experiments

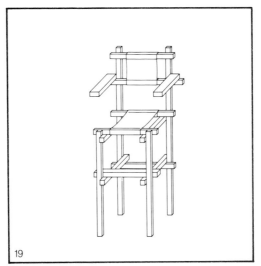

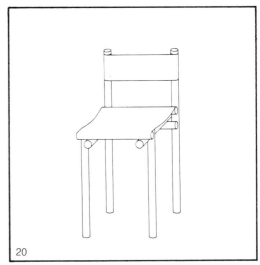

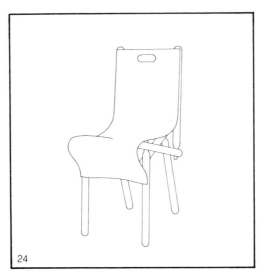

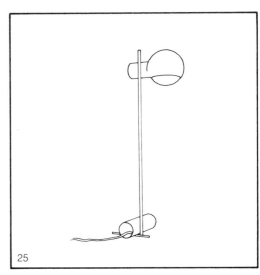

19. Kinderstoel, 1920.
20. Pianostoel, 1923.
21. Stoel, 1924.
22. Stoel, 1925.
23. Kinderstoel, after 1923.
24. Stoel, c. 1927, built of round natural wood billets and leather seat.
25. Tafellamp, 1925.

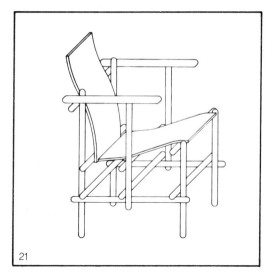

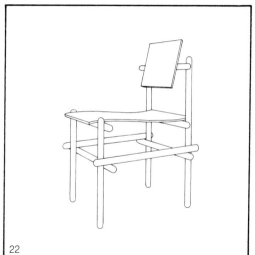

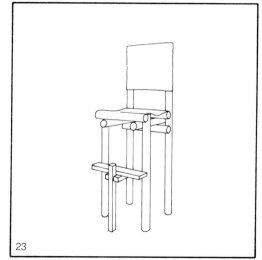

7.   KINDERSTOEL (Baby chair), 1920.
Deal structure, lacquered red with white terminals;
seat and back of natural leather; 45×40×90 cm.

Exh.:   Amsterdam, 1971; London, 1972.

Coll.:   Amsterdam, Stedelijk Museum.

*The structure is similar to that of the ''Rood Blauwe''
and ''Hoge stoel,'' and even the thickness of the
quadrangular listel is the same; only the footrest bar is
wider than the others and corresponds to the width of
the arms. Viewed as a whole, it is much more slender
and simplified than the two 1919 chairs, and the
traditional rigid planes of the seat and back are
replaced here by stretched leather.
The execution also may be presumed to be the work of
Rietveld.*

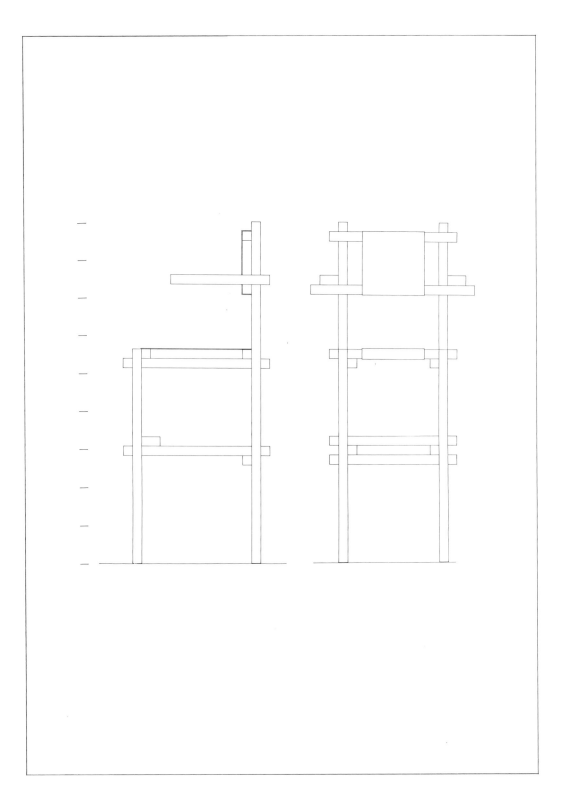

8.   PIANOSTOEL (Piano stool), 1923.
Structure of mahogany wooden billets dyed with
mordant and spirit polished; terminals dyed violet;
seat and back in brown leather; 35×36×75 cm.

Exh.: Utrecht, 1958; Amsterdam, 1971; London, 1972.

Repr.:   Bouwkundig Weekblad, 1924; El Lissitzky,
1926; *De 8 en Opbouw*, 1935; W. Sandberg, 1957; *Cat.
G. Rietveld architect*, 1971.

Coll.:   Amsterdam, Stedelijk Museum.

*Its name indicates that this seat was meant to
accompany a piano. Here for the first time Rietveld
replaced the quadrangular listel with a billet having a
diameter of 35 mm.; the greatest technical difficulty
from the point of view of assembly was that of joining
the tangential points which did not hold easily. It was
placed in the Schröder Huis.*
*Rietveld also made a variant of this seat as a baby
chair.*

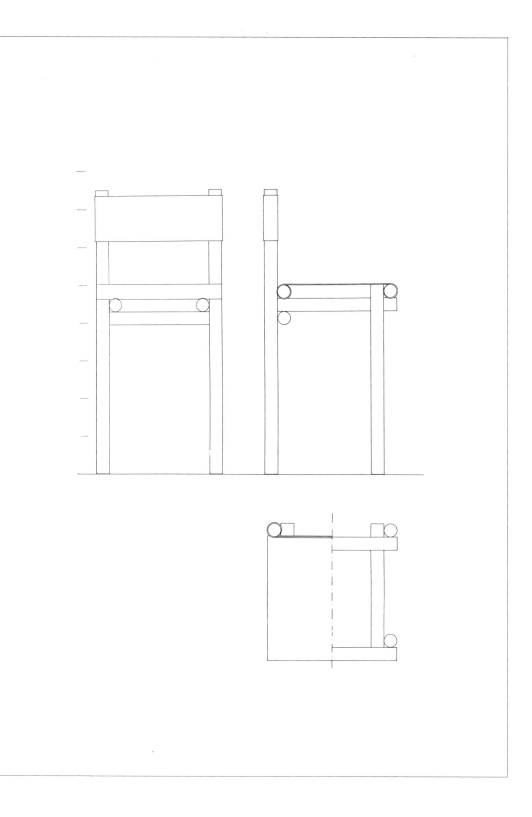

The piano stool in the version of a baby's high chair.

9. STOEL (Easy chair), 1924.
Structure of ebonized wooden billets having a
diameter of 30 mm.; seat and back of curved plywood
with leather; 65×65×94 cm.

Exh.: Utrecht, 1958; Amsterdam, 1971; London,
1972.

Repr.: *L'architecture vivante*, 1925; W. van der
Pluym, 1954; T. M. Brown, 1958; *Cat. G. Rietveld
architect*, 1971.

Coll.: Utrecht, Centraal Museum; Utrecht, Schröder
Huis.

*The supporting structure is very similar to that of the
"Rood Blauwe" but differs from the latter by its use of
wooden billets, with rounded ends and the anatomical
line imprinted on the seat and back; a version with less
sloping seat and back than in the more famous model
gives a chair suited to a more upright position. It was
designed for the Schröder Huis.*

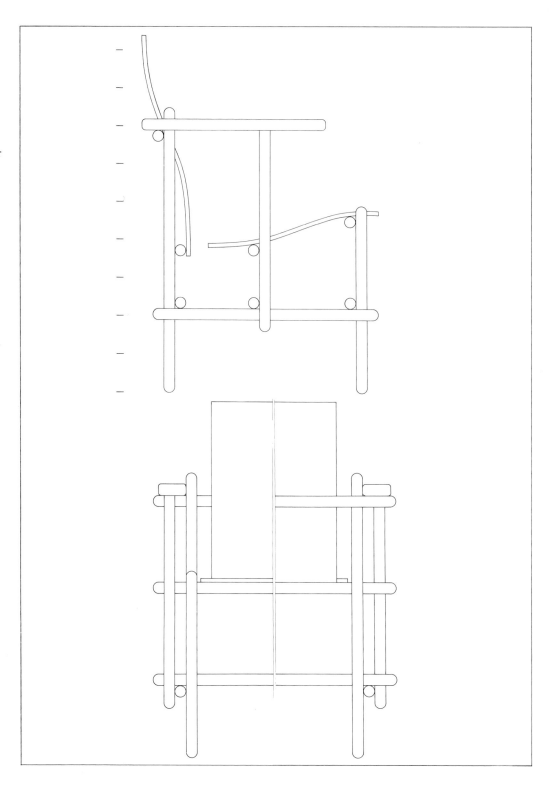

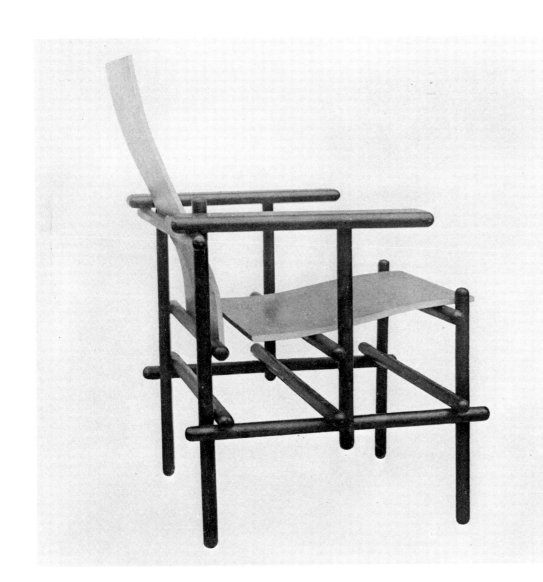

Rietveld photographed in 1927, showing in the foreground the Birza-fauteuil and the chair on the left.

10. TAFELLAMP (Table lamp), 1925.
Made of metal tubing varnished black, red, and blue; spherical bulb painted black over most of its surface; 15×20×36 cm.

Exh.: Utrecht, 1958; Rome, 1967; Amsterdam, 1971; London, 1972.

Repr.: El Lissitzky, 1926; A. H. Barr, 1954; T. M. Brown, 1958; P. Overy, 1969.

Coll.: Amsterdam, Stedelijk Museum; New York, Museum of Modern Art.

This very simple lamp has a design based entirely on geometrical balance; a very interesting feature is the Cartesian node solution with tubes of various lengths and different diameters; at the top and tangential to the vertical tube the lampholder was placed as a perpendicular counterweight to the predominant part of the base; the upper part of the lamp is varnished black so as to produce a greater concentration of light. This lamp was inserted into the radio apparatus designed by Rietveld in the same year. In order to show the whole mechanism of the radio, including a latch system which enabled him to vary its position, Rietveld placed it inside a glass case. The apparatus was destroyed and never rebuilt.

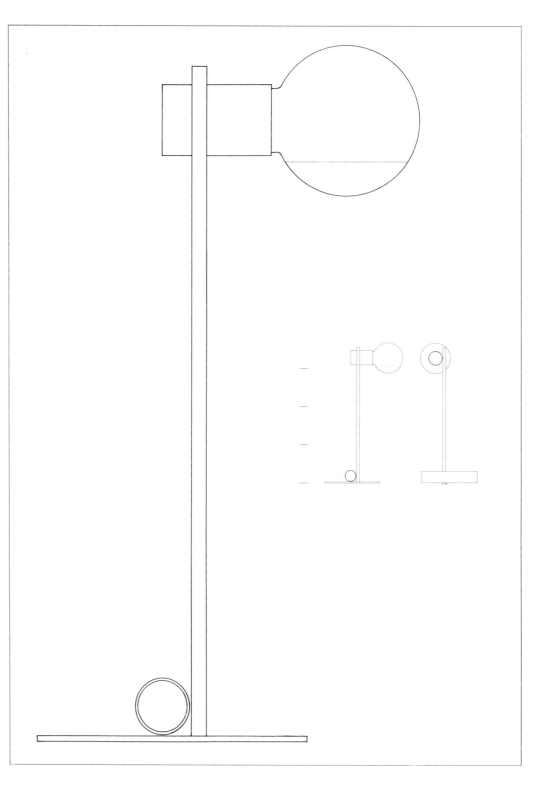

On the previous page, left: *glass case with radio and latch system, published in* De Stijl, *nos. 75, 76, 1926-27;* below, this page: *original sketch for the design.*

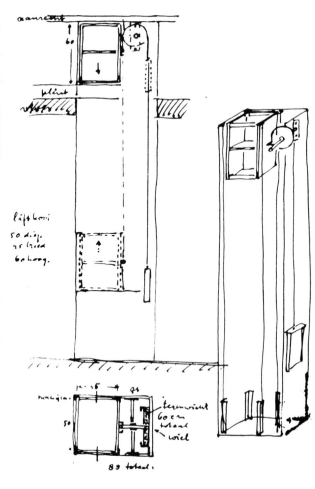

The "Military" Series

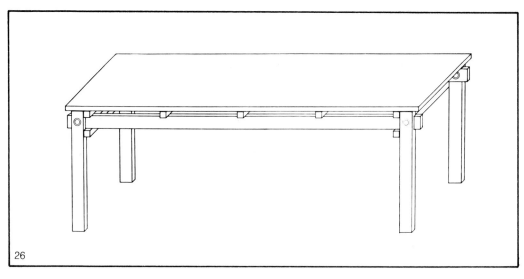

26

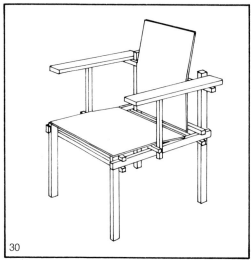

30

26. *Militaire tafel, 1923.*
27. *Militaire stoel, 1923.*
28. *Militaire tafeltje, 1923.*
29. *Militair krukje, 1924.*
30. *Armstoel, 1925.*

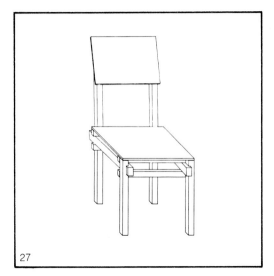

27

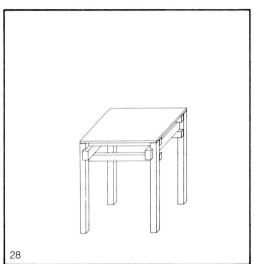

28

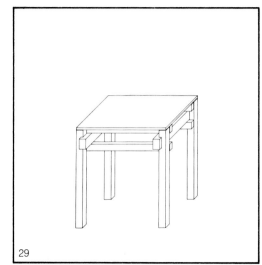

29

71

11. MILITAIRE STOEL (Military chair), 1923.
Structure in ebonized oak with terminals lacquered
white; seat and back lacquered white; there exists also
a version lacquered white all over, with black
terminals; 39×52×91 cm.

Exh.: Utrecht, 1958; Rome, 1967; Amsterdam, 1971;
London, 1972.

Repr.: *De Stijl*, 1926; El Lissitzky, 1926; W.
Sandberg, 1957; T. M. Brown, 1958; H. L. C. Jaffé,
1967; *Cat. G. Rietveld architect*, 1971.

Coll.: Amsterdam, Stedeiijk Museum; Utrecht,
Schröder Huis.

*This chair, which can be taken to pieces, was ordered
from Rietveld by a military club. Unlike the "Rood
Blauwe," the uprights are here not connected by way
of juxtaposition but by a half-groove which serves to
strengthen the hold. The metal hinges complete the
welding of the various parts. The model with
rectangular section is without doubt less elegant than
the quadrangular. In the year following the design, the
chair was placed in thè Schröder Huis.
The replicas were executed by G. van de Groenekan.*

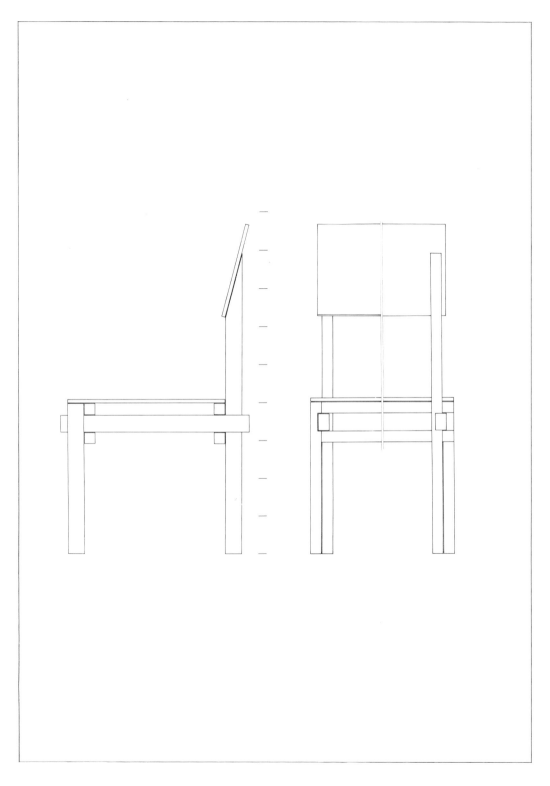

The chair published in De Stijl, *nos. 75, 76, 1926-7.*

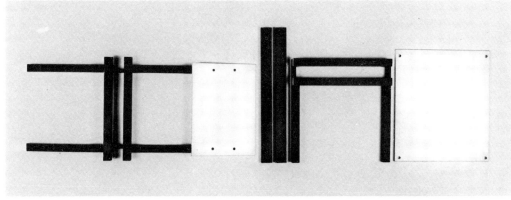

The various parts ready for assembly.   73

12. MILITAIRE TAFEL (Military table), 1923.
In wood lacquered white with black terminals;
83 × 200 × 70 cm.

Exh.:   Utrecht, 1958; Amsterdam, 1971; London,
1972.

Repr.:   T. M. Brown, 1958.

Coll.:   Amsterdam, Stedelijk Museum.

Constructed at the same time as the "Militaire stoel"
and possibly commissioned by the same military club.
The constructive principles are the same and only the
size of the supporting structure has been increased.
Rietveld placed it in the Schröder Huis, representing it
already as one of the axonometries designed by him as
a part of the whole, as a fundamental object in the
structuring of the interior.

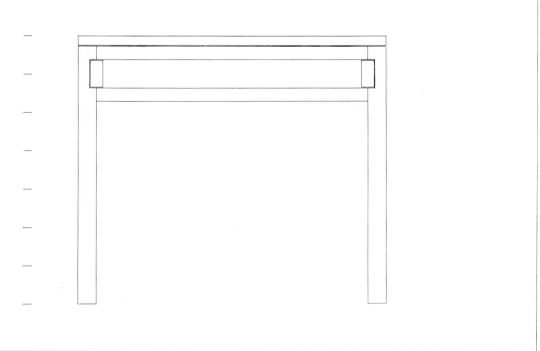

13., 14. KRUKJE – TAFELTJE (Stool, Small table),
1923-24.
Structure in ebonized wood with terminal lacquered
white; resting surface lacquered white; 39×39×43
cm.; 39×44×45 cm.

Exh.: Utrecht, 1958; Rome, 1967; Amsterdam, 1971;
London, 1972.

Repr.: Cat. G. Rietveld architect, 1971.

Coll.: Amsterdam, Stedelijk Museum; Utrecht,
Schröder Huis; Otterloo, Kroller-Müller Museum.

*The structure in both cases reflects that of the chair,
and only the total size is varied.*

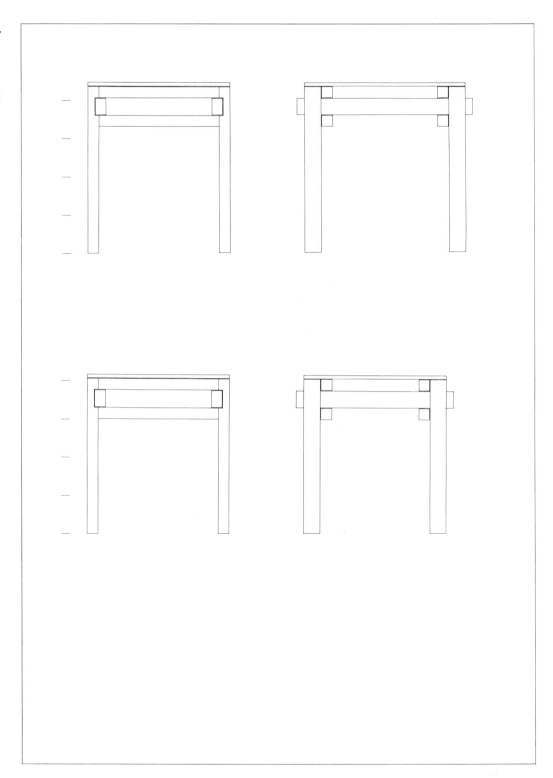

15.   ARMSTOEL (Armchair), 1925.
In wood, lacquered red with white terminals. A version painted white all over has also been made; 62×63×94 cm.

Exh.:   Utrecht, 1958; Rome, 1967; Amsterdam, 1971; London, 1972.

Repr.:   T. M. Brown, 1958; *Cat. G. Rietveld architect*, 1971.

Coll.:   Amsterdam, Stedelijk Museum.

Known also as the chair with flexibile seat. The design followed the same principles of composition as in the "Militaire stoel," but in the armchair version; particularly interesting features are the flexible seat and back which curve over a central crossbar.
In this chair Rietveld has so lightened the structure as to reduce it to the indispensable, so leading the way to his future metal chairs on which he began to work the next year.
It was put inside the Schröder Huis.

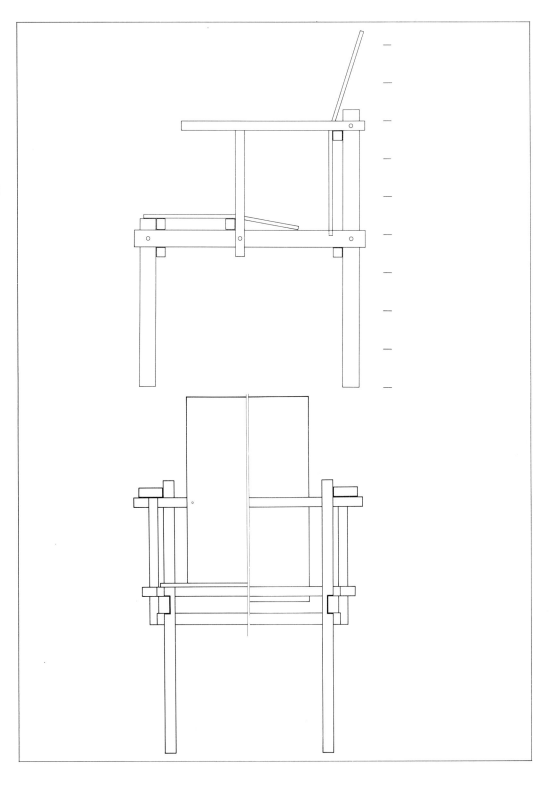

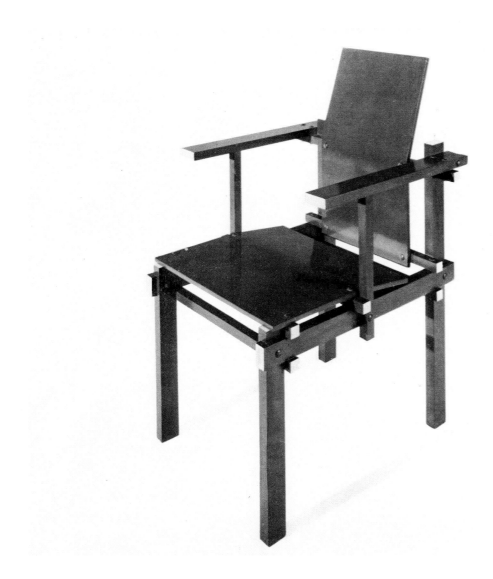

Structural Affinity between Object and Environment

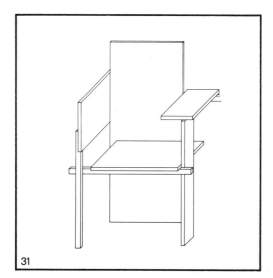

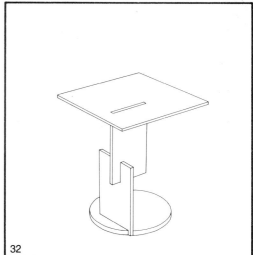

31. Berlijnse stoel, 1923.
32. Divantafeltje, 1923.

31

32

G. Rietveld, Schröder Huis, 1924, design for the interior.

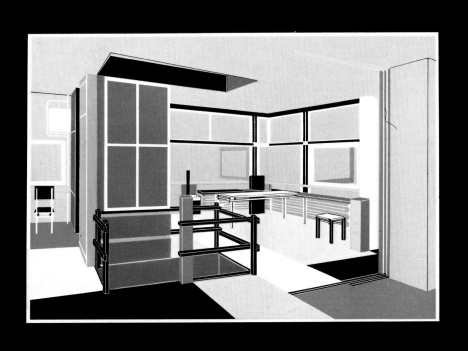

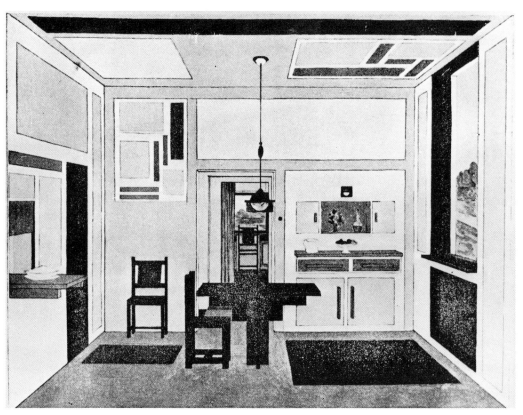

The first neoplastic interior, created by Van Doesburg and furnished by Rietveld, published in De Stijl, no. 12, 1920; above right: V. Huszar, Form-color-composition in a room, 1921; below right: Huszar and Rietveld, design of a room for the 1923 Berlin exhibition.

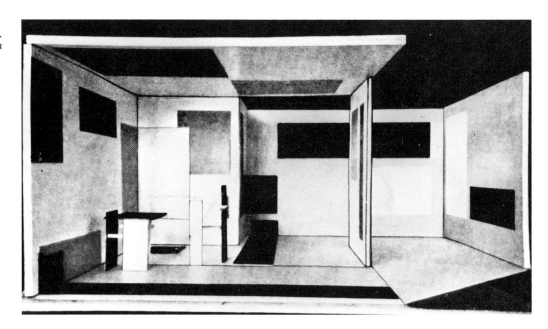

There have been various examples of the relationship between object and environment in the history of modern architecture: the Peacock Room by James Whistler decorated in 1876–77; the Red House by William Morris; or the much more modest Dijsselhofkamer, the room designed by Gerrit William Dijsselhof (1866–1924) which reduces to a petit bourgeois level the gaudiness of the Peacock Room. Constructed with obvious reference to the batik decoration of Japanese art, this room to some extent came to represent the symbol of Dutch art nouveau.[1] One must not forget the work of Mackintosh, who did not neglect any detail in the relationship between object and environment; a sufficient example is the Hill House in Helensburgh (1902).

But the members of De Stijl adopted a more peremptory approach in this sphere. As the theories of neoplasticism gradually became consolidated, its protagonists often passed from the two-dimensional plane of the picture to the spatial field, until they encompassed architectonic elements, showing ever more clearly their demand for a neoplastic environment by way of which they could attain to the realization of the neoplastic city which they considered the culmination of universal order. This tendency emerged at the early stages, as can be seen from the house designed in 1919 by Van Doesburg and furnished by Rietveld.[2] An important contribution relating to the matter under consideration was the design for a room by Vilmos Huszar (1921). Van Doesburg wrote in *De Stijl* about this design: "The effect of the colors in their spatial relationship, the unity of furniture, hangings, carpets, have been so harmoniously balanced one with the other in the execution of this design that the result is not only aesthetic, but ethical as well."[3] Here the relationships between the objects and the painted surfaces which delimit the room develop in a greater rhythmical tension and are integrated in a more penetrating way.

Also of the year 1921 was the study by the German Max Burchartz[4] for an interior painted all over, but no architectural features were introduced into the interior which consisted of a cube box painted on the inside and divided by a sequence of two-dimensional painted walls. Mondrian fell into the same two-dimensionalism in 1927 when he designed the *Salon de Madame B.*[5]

Mondrian's "room" is one of the two of his designs which pass the barrier of the painting's surface to virtually invest space, although by means of the relationship of plastic forces he always sought for a single spatial unity in his paintings. The other design, which is not so well known as the first, consists of three stage sets for the play *L'éphemère est éternel*, written by Mondrian's friend Michel Seuphor in 1926. However, Mondrian still retained a two-dimensional environment and even in the *Salon de Madame B.* he confined himself to painting the six surfaces of the cube box with rectangles in primary colors, placed one beside the other, without the grill pattern of black lines which was so characteristic of his painting after 1920–21. He then added to it, in rigorously geometrical terms, a bed and small elliptical table. This last feature must be considered the only nonrectilineal expression in his structural vocabulary, at least from the time when he finally abandoned the cubist phase. Very different were the theoretical studies concerned with spatial relationships carried out after 1921 by Van Doesburg and Van Eesteren, joined soon afterward by Rietveld, who was responsible for most of the maquettes which were the visual embodiment of their ideas. These followed a similar line to that already adopted by the painters of the group, but in their approach to the question of spatialism they followed an inverse process to that of the architectural tradition: the breaking down of volumes from which to set off again for new articulated structures.

Bruno Zevi, for whom "the syntax of four-dimensional de-composition" was the central invariable of the modern style of architecture, wrote concerning this phase of De Stijl's development: "Contrasting with the traditional method of first drawing the ground plan, then the sections, and then the façades, to conclude in pictorial perspectives, that is, contrasting with a norm which, through two-dimensional stages, finally actuates an inert three-dimensionality of a boxlike nature attained by the mechanical joining together of floors, walls, and roof, here the volumes, full and empty, are broken up into slabs, then reassembled in a tripody of dissonant recesses. . . . Now, examine the wall sections: they are no longer 'walls,' they have no weight, they can be dismembered into smaller rectangles, distinguished in color by the basic colors of blue, red, yellow, white, and black. To experience this dynamic process, the making of the work in time, is to define its coherence in an essential invariable of the modern style: the breaking up of spaces, volumes, and planes, or more exactly, of volumes into freely arranged slabs."[6]

The theoretical phase of De Stijl architecture ended and crystallized in the 1923 Paris exhibition held in Léonce Rosenberg's Galerie L'Effort Moderne. But it was exemplified in a concrete form immediately afterward by Rietveld. An early example of the transposition from the field of theory to practice occurred when Rietveld worked together with Huszar on a semipermanent building for an exhibition pavilion in Berlin in 1923. This was a most important collaboration because it showed the close affinity of ideas between the two architects and also because of the equilibrium they achieved between the architectural environment, the pictorial aspect, and the other elements, all in a solution of rhythmical and chromatic continuity. This was 1923, and apart from his participation in the Weimar exhibition, to which we have referred, Rietveld worked together with Van Doesburg and Van Eesteren. He collaborated with Huszar in this model of a pavilion for the Berlin exhibition, and placed in it also a new chair, later given the name of "Berlijnse stoel" because of this association.

The exhibition area was treated with a simple plasticity: it consisted of a perimeter following the line of the Cartesian axes, interrupted by a single wall supporting a partial roof; all the surfaces were covered with rectangular blocks of color creating new planes or apparent and unreal windows, so contributing to the definition of the spatial field.

Huszar's pictorial contribution reflects his preceding compositions: broad zones of color juxtaposed dynamically without being intersected by the black lines which were typical of the paintings of Mondrian and Van Doesburg; in fact it could be said that the lines are formed as negatives in the spaces interposed between one block and another.

In perfect harmony with the surrounding area the new chair emerges from the floor. It has been designed according to the same principles found in the earlier theoretical phase, but with the function of completing and emphasizing the room itself and imbuing it with the significance of the spatial dimension.

The "Berlijnse stoel" is to be considered the first stage in a new metamorphosis which Rietveld imposed on his chairs from this time onward. He went beyond the method he had previously adopted of constructing by means of lines: the chair became more enclosed, like a small building; the legs, which for centuries in the history of this object had supported the seat, were eliminated, and replaced by other planes or by asymmetrical structures, free-standing in space and forming a rhythmical pattern and meticulous equilibrium between verticals and horizontals. It was a method of constructing by planes instead of by lines. The chair was painted in various shades of gray so that it became a neutral object, in contrast to the bright primary colors produced by the room itself.

The Schröder Huis

The experience he gained when he worked together with Huszar on the "Berlin pavilion," as well as his collaboration with Van Doesburg and Van Eesteren in the making of the small models for their architectural designs, led Rietveld to a degree of maturity which gave him the confidence to design a building for the first time, that is, a work of architecture which was not of a temporary or semipermanant nature such as an exhibition

84

T. van Doesburg, design for a wall with elementarist paintings in the cinema-cabaret L'Aubette, Strasbourg, 1927.

M. Burchartz, study of color applied to a room, 1921.

Right: *P. Mondrian, design for the* Salon de Madame B., *1927.*

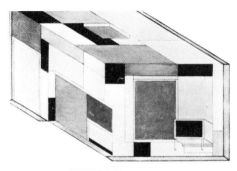

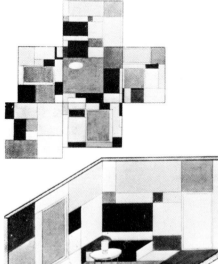

pavilion, but a permanent work of architecture with all the structural implications associated with such a concept. In the small house on Prins Hendriklaan, Utrecht, he put into operation all the technique he had assimilated up to that time, not the least important part of which was what he had learned from his work with chairs, especially the "Rood Blauwe" and "Berlijnse stoel." He was able to demonstrate the validity of the iconographic significance of these objects, used as a large-scale projection into the architectural sphere. The path taken by Rietveld led him from the object to the work of architecture, using the same method of design.

The house was constructed by germination from within, following the Cartesian axes, and projected through slabs and planes on to the exterior. Rietveld employed the logic of geometry, exploiting its laws to the tiniest fraction and to their farthest consequences, and starting off from this point to reconstruct the whole in perfect harmony, just as in nature a biochemical chain is formed from its most simple and elementary components.[7]

The house is built mainly of brick, with the foundations and balconies of concrete. Numerous visible girders in painted steel, with "I" section, follow a vertical and a horizontal direction over all the external sides, crisscrossed according to the same structural principle as found in the "Rood Blauwe" and his other first chairs. The planes which form the walls, windows, and roof exist autonomously in space. The broad transparent surfaces, the corner windows, make it possible to project the interior decor onto the exterior and at the same time bring the garden and surrounding countryside into the building. The land around the house seems to continue inside it because of these transparent walls. In the eastern corner at the upper level where two windows meet Rietveld deliberately moved back the supporting beam of the corner, so creating a most unexpected visual effect; when the two windows are opened, the corner disappears completely, substantially modifying the interrelationship of planes and volumes. The apparently fragile equilibrium of the house is a determining factor in its elegance. The house faces southeast and when it was built it was the last house on the outskirts of Utrecht; now unfortunately it is submerged and hidden by an overhead highway.[8]

The Concept of Space

The box-shaped building contains two superimposed living areas each measuring about 60 square meters in surface. It may be considered one of the first examples of open plan housing where the various zones can be separated only by means of sliding partitions which follow a precise route indicated by colored surfaces. Otherwise, only the position of the objects, whether furniture or utensils, and the activity of the occupant, will define the function of each of its parts. Even the objects, in their structural development, become space.[9]

The arrangement of the activities in the Schröder Huis is entirely unexpected: the influence of Wright has been shaken off, with the "day areas"—living room, study, dining room, and kitchen—being quite separate and distinct from the "night areas"—bedrooms and bathrooms. In Rietveld's house all the areas were intermingled, integrated, and concatenated without distinction, with a spatial continuity clearly maintained throughout. It is clear that for Rietveld spatialism was of essential importance, and the great emphasis given to this aspect must be considered one of the prerogatives of De Stijl architecture. But what was the nature of the concept of space he could have acquired at that time? We may perhaps find it in the words of Vantongerloo, writing during those years: "Ever since man has moved, he has had the concept of space. Our senses imply the notion of it. Without our senses it is obvious that we would have no need of it. Space is useful to us in order to situate objects. Space is indispensable to us, even if we cannot define it, it is inseparable from life itself. We cannot conceive of existence without space."[10] And

Model reconstruction of the Schröder Huis for the exhibition Rietveld Schröder Huis 1925-1975.

Opposite: the technical layouts for the construction of the house, drawn by Rietveld.
His collaborator was Truus Schröder-Schräder.

Rietveld's sketch of the northeast side of the Schröder Huis, 1924.

Rietveld himself said much later (1957): "If for a particular purpose we separate, limit, and reduce to a human scale any part of limitless space, this becomes a piece of space created as a reality. In this way, a segment of space has been absorbed by our human system."[11]

These words seem to exemplify a particular way of envisaging space with the mentality of the 1930s. Here is another example: "When we construct, all we do is to take out from natural space a suitable amount of space, enclose it and protect it, and the whole of architecture is born from this necessity."[12] But as we have seen, there can be far more complex implications which make space into the center of gravity of a cosmic system. In an effort to find a new way of envisaging architecture, Berlage had written as early as 1908: "The art of the builder consists in this: the creation of space, not the design of façades. A spatial envelope is created by means of walls so that one space leading onto a sequence of spaces is defined according to the complexity of the walls."[13] But space as understood by De Stijl was an infinite and abstract space, and the concept of *Raum*, the circumscribed space described by Berlage, had been long superseded.

As is well known, the two fundamental concepts of space according to modern ideas are first the perspective view belonging to the Renaissance and second the Cartesian view. The De Stijl architects immediately rejected the illusionistic, symbolical, and psychological qualities of perspective and operated within Cartesian space, which is both realistic and abstract at the same time. In his Schröder Huis Rietveld evolved an image of space based on de-composition and analysis. His interpretation of Cartesian space here, however, was far removed from the illuminist approach and it is not impossible that it was partly influenced by Schoenmaekers' plastic mathematics.

Rietveld's method of composition with the use of slabs therefore corresponds to the analytical, positivist, and de-compositive mentality and to an increase of communication with the external world—it makes it possible for the whole effect to be experienced in a kinetic and simultaneous view.

The same may be said of this house as was said by Marcolli in relation to the design for a villa by Mies (1923). Here too the internal slabs (consisting of sliding walls instead of wall sectors) "run like a number of coordinates which from Cartesian axes are transformed into lines of force, vehicles for space, and which multiply and displace continuously the point of origin of the axes, creating a whole variation of points of observation of space."[14] Space is dilated and multiplied, continually creating new points of observation; the living area becomes pure spatialism, pure abstraction.

Today problems relating to space have been greatly amplified, especially through the studies of Gestalt psychology, which not only treats space as a factor of communication, but examines the processes of the configuration and "image" of space itself. "Objects, structures, and signs, insofar as they are images which occupy the visual world, possess a spatialism in the sense that when they are organized in one way rather than another, they form one kind of space rather than another."[15] From this viewpoint problems of space are mainly those of direction, orientation, distance, and depth. It is emphasized that all animals are surrounded by spheres of intimacy and sociality; this is the case for man too, who possesses visual spheres, olfactory spheres, tactile spheres, and hence spatial spheres, of which he is not always aware. According to the Gestalt psychologists, what the brain receives is a message concerning muscular expansions and contractions which occur when the hand touches the object or explores its surface. As I pass through a room my brain is being informed of a series of leg movements which follow each other in time; in such sensations no space is "contained"; in order to be able to

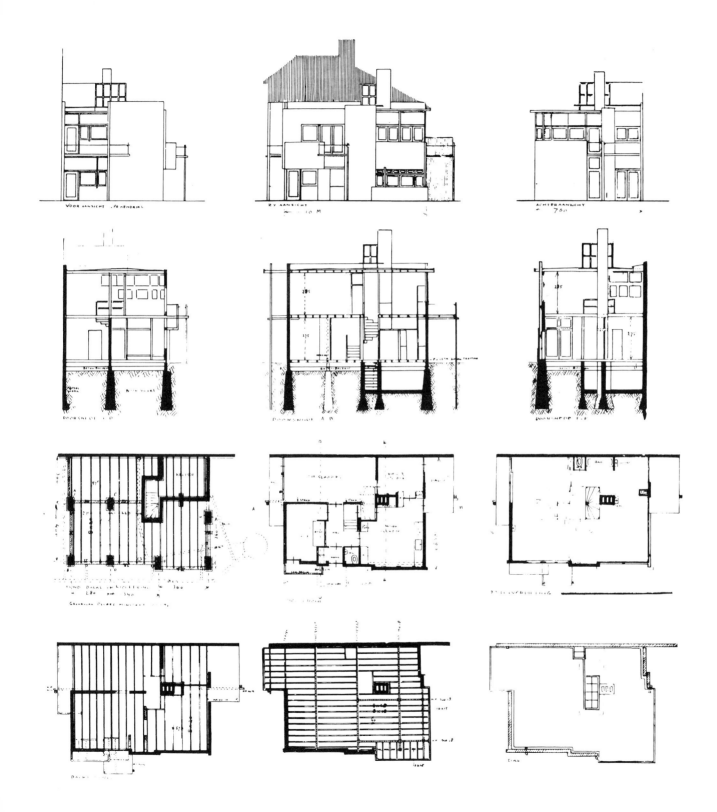

Left: *the Schröder Huis after the 1974 restoration;* below: *one of the first pictures of the house published after its completion.*

Schröder Huis. View of the living room. Photograph published in De Stijl, *no. 12, 1925.*

experience space kinaesthetically, the brain must build it up within itself out of sensorial messages which are not spatial; in other words, the same task exists for kinaesthesia as for vision, except that it seems more difficult to realize how this occurs. There is no doubt that sensations deriving from the organs of touch, from the muscles, joints and tendons, play a large part in giving us an awareness of space.[16]

There exist also cultural differences in the perception of space; Western man, for example, experiences space as a gap between objects, whereas the Japanese, who have a strong sense of space, experience it as a form among other forms, capable of being given an autonomous architectural shape. This "Japanese-like" sense of space had been arrived at by the architecture of De Stijl by intuition, without forming part of a formulated theory.

After the architecture of De Stijl had taken concrete form in the construction of the Schröder Huis, that is, after its passage from theory to practice, Van Doesburg was able to define his *Basic Principles of Neoplastic Architecture*.[17] But before we go on to examine these seventeen points of the new architecture, we should pause to consider one of the aspects which distinguishes De Stijl from other movements: the use of color in architecture, viewed as a spatial entity.

The use of color was to represent the basic contribution toward delimiting and interpenetrating the various planes plastically. The concept of the simultaneity of a global vision, which had originated in cubism, was here carried further. Van Doesburg said of color in 1928: "Spatial design could not be imaginable without light. . . . The architectural design of light is impossible without color. . . . Without color, architecture is expressionless and blind. . . . In modern architecture the surfaces ask to be animated, in other words, composed with the aid of pure color, the color of space. And even apart from any surface coloring, the appropriate use of modern materials is subject to the same laws as colors in space and time. Just as the various colors (red, blue, and yellow, for example) each represent a special energy, so too modern materials (cement, iron, and glass, for example) each represent a special force. Blue and yellow form two absolutely opposed energies, and I call this opposition 'tension.' A similar tension is produced by two materials, iron and glass. The evaluation of these tensions in space and time is just as 'aesthetic' and architectonic as the evaluation of the two colors on a surface or in space."[18]

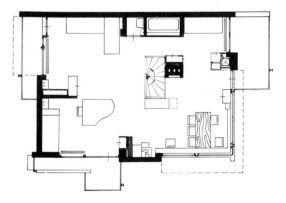

Ground plans showing the upper floor, respectively enclosed by the sliding walls, and open; below: plan of the ground floor.

The Seventeen Points of Neoplastic Architecture

1. Form. Instead of taking a preconceived form as a starting point, the modern architect poses the problem of construction for each project. Form is born *a posteriori*.

2. Elements. The new architecture is elementary, that is to say, it develops out of the constructive elements: light, function, materials, volume, time, space, color. These basic elements are the creative elements at the same time.

3. Economy. The new architecture is economical in that it employs the most elementary and essential instruments without wasting any means or materials.

4. Function. The new architecture is functional, that is, it is based on a synthesis of all the practical requirements. The architect determines it at a clear and easily understood level.

5. Shapelessness. The new architecture is "shapeless," but well-determined. It does not follow previously determined lines or act as a kind of mold into which the functional spaces are to be poured. Unlike all the styles of the past, the new architectural methodology does not recognize fundamental and immutable types. The division and subdivision of the internal and external spaces are determined in a rigid way by means of planes which do not possess an individual form. Through this determination of the planes,

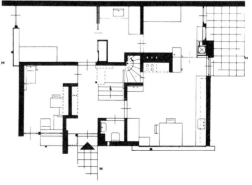

89

Stapelkast, small cupboard with separate sections, designed by Rietveld for the Schröder Huis.

these can be extended to infinity on all sides and without interruptions. This results in a coordinated system in which the various points correspond to an equal number of points in universal space; this is why there exists a relationship between the various planes and the external space.

6. *The monumental.* Instead of being monumental, the new architecture is rather an architecture in transformation, light and transparent. It has dissociated the idea of the monumental from the "large" and the "small"; it shows that everything exists in relation to something else.

7. *The void.* The new architecture knows no points of passivity: it has conquered the void. The window is no longer a hole in the wall. The window assumes an active importance in relation to the position of the flat and blind surface of the wall. An aperture, a void, is not born out of nothingness because everything is rigorously determined by contrast.

8. *The ground plan.* The new architecture has pierced the wall by suppressing the duality between exterior and interior. Walls no longer have a supporting function but have become resting points. This creates an open plan, quite different from those of classical architecture, because here the spaces of the interior and exterior interpenetrate each other.

9. *Subdivision.* The new architecture is open instead of closed. As a whole it consists of a general area subdivided into various areas related to the function of the living area. This subdivision occurs through separating planes (internal) and wall surfaces (external). The former, which separate the functional areas, can even be furniture; in other words, they can be replaced by sliding sections (among which we can list doors). In a later stage in the development of modern architecture, the ground plan will disappear. The spatial composition designed on two dimensions by means of a horizontal section (the ground plan) can be replaced by an exact calculation of the construction. We shall no longer be able to make use of Euclidean geometry, but the whole will be made easier by the use of four-dimensional non-Euclidean geometries.

10. *Time.* The new architecture is not measured by space alone, but also by time viewed as an architectonic value. The units of space and time confer a new and plastically more complete aspect to the architectonic whole. This is what we call "an animated space."

11. *Plastic aspect.* Fourth dimension of space-time.

12. *Static aspect.* The new architecture is anticubic, which means that the various spaces are not held within an enclosed cube. Instead, the various space cells (including the volumes of the balconies) develop in an eccentric direction from the center to the periphery of the cube, with the result that the dimensions of height, width, and depth assume a new plastic expression. The modern house will thus convey an impression of gliding or hovering in the air, contrary to the laws of gravity.

13. *Symmetry and repetition.* The new architecture has done away with monotonous repetition and destroyed the equality between the two halves, or symmetry. It recognizes no repetition in duration, no "wall overlooking the street," and no norms. A block of houses is a total entity, as is an independent house. The same laws are valid for both. Equilibrium and symmetry are very different things. Instead of symmetry, the new architecture proposes: *an equilibrial relationship of unequal parts,* that is, parts which are different (in position, size, proportion, etc.) for their functional character. The conformity of these parts is determined by the equilibrium of nonconformity and not by equality. The new architecture makes no distinction between "front" and "back," "left" side and "right" side, and if possible not even "upper" and "lower."

14. *Frontalism.* Frontalism arrives out of a static conception of life; the new architecture will be enriched through a plastic and polyhedric development in space-time.

15. *Color.* The new architecture has done away with the individual expressiveness of painting—that is, the picture as an imaginary and illusory expression of

harmony—indirectly by means of naturalistic forms, or more directly, by the method of constructing through colored planes. The new architecture draws color into itself organically. Color is one of the elementary means of making the harmony of architectonic relationships visible. Without color, these proportional relationships are not a living reality, and it is through the medium of color that architecture becomes the fulfilment of all plastic research, whether in space or in time. In a neutral and colorless architecture, the equilibrium of the relationships among the architectonic elements remains invisible. This is why another element has been introduced to bring them together: a painting (on a wall) or a sculpture in space. But these always represented a dualism associated with a period in which the aesthetic life and real life were kept apart. For a long time the abolition of this dualism had been the objective of all artists. When modern architecture was born, the painter-constructor found his true sphere of creation. He aesthetically organizes color in space-time and plastically reveals a new dimension.

16. *Decoration.* The new architecture is antidecorative. Instead of rendering the plane surface more dramatic, instead of being a superficial ornament, color is, like light, an elementary means of expression of a purely architectonic nature.

17. *Architecture as a synthesis of the new plastic construction.* In the new conception of architecture, the structure of the building is subordinated. And it is only through a convergence of all the plastic arts that architecture can be considered complete. The neoplastic artist is convinced that he is building in the field of space-time, and this implies a readiness to journey into the four dimensions of space-time, since the new architecture concedes nothing to the imagination (in the form of a picture or sculpture separable from the whole). The aim is to create first and foremost a harmony, using only the means inherent in discipline. Each architectonic element contributes to the creation of a maximum of plastic expression, on a logical and practical basis.

On another occasion, Van Doesburg wrote: "The house has been dismembered and sectioned in its plastic elements. The static axis of the old construction has been destroyed: the house has thus become an object which offers all its sides without preference to the spectator's passage."

When these ideas had been promulgated, it could be seen that the Schröder Huis by Rietveld was a living embodiment of them and it remains a visual manifesto of the correct method of building according to neoplasticism.

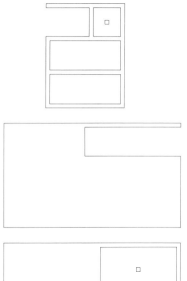

G. Rietveld (with T. Schröder), bedroom in the Weteringschans House, Amsterdam, 1926; relief drawing of the small article of furniture which appears in the photo.

[1] Reconstructed, on permanent exhibition in the Gemeente Museum, The Hague.
[2] Published in *De Stijl*, III, 12 (November 1920).
[3] Theo van Doesburg, in *De Stijl*, V, 1 (January 1922).
[4] Published in *De Stijl*, V, 12 (December 1922).
[5] It is presumed that the project was inspired by Madame Blatavsky, the founder of the International Theosophical Society, to which Mondrian belonged.
[6] Bruno Zevi, *Poetica dell'architettura neoplastica*.
[7] Rietveld was helped in the designing of the house by Truus Schröder-Schräder who commissioned it and at the same time worked together with him on it. This collaboration began in 1921 and continued until the early 1940s, for nearly all the building projects undertaken by Rietveld.
[8] Many critics consider the Schröder Huis to be the first ideologically modern house after those built by Wright and Loos; the first to be considered a "liberated dwelling." It preceded by a year the

buildings in Dessau designed by Gropius for the Bauhaus teachers; by three years those in Stuttgart by Oud, Mies, and others; and by four years the Villa Savoye by Le Corbusier. For an analytical interpretation see the catalogue to the exhibition "Rietveld Schröder Huis 1925-1975," Centraal Museum, Utrecht, (March-May 1975).
[9] To verify the validity of the structural principles in relation to the order which results from them, and to explore further the concepts of "order" and "disorder" in relation to the creative process, see Rudolf Arnheim, *Entropy and Art: An Essay on Disorder and Order.*
[10] Georges Vantongerloo, *L'art et son avenir.*
[11] Quoted in the catalogue to "G. Rietveld architect," Stedelijk Museum, Amsterdam (1971).
[12] Geoffrey Scott, *L'architettura dell'Umanesimo* (Bari, 1939).
[13] H. Petrus Berlage, *Grundlagen und Entwicklung der*

Architektur (1908).
[14] Attilio Marcolli, *Teoria del campo* (Florence, 1971).
[15] Ibid.
[16] Rudolf Arnheim, *Art and Visual Perception: A Psychology of the Creative Eye* (Berkeley, 1954).
[17] 1925, later integrated in 1930.
[18] Bruno Zevi, in *Poetica dell'architettura neoplastica*.

16.   BERLIJNSE STOEL (Berlin chair), 1923.
In deal lacquered black, medium gray, and light gray;
74 × 58 × 106 cm.

Exh.:   Berlin, 1923; Utrecht, 1958; Rome, 1967;
Amsterdam, 1971; London, 1972; Zürich, 1973.

Repr.:   *L'architecture vivante*, 1923; A. H. Jansen,
1925; Lissitzky & Arp, 1925; Holland, "Sier-en . . ."
1927; *Vouloir*, 1927; W. Sandberg, 1957; T. M. Brown,
1958; *Architectural Design*, 1965; P. Overy, 1969;
"Die Zwanziger Jahre . . ." 1973; C. Meadmore,
1974; "Rietveld Schröder Huis . . ." 1975.

Coll.:   Amsterdam, Stedelijk Museum; Utrecht,
Schröder Huis.

*Designed for exhibition in the Dutch pavilion at the
1923 Berlin exhibition.*

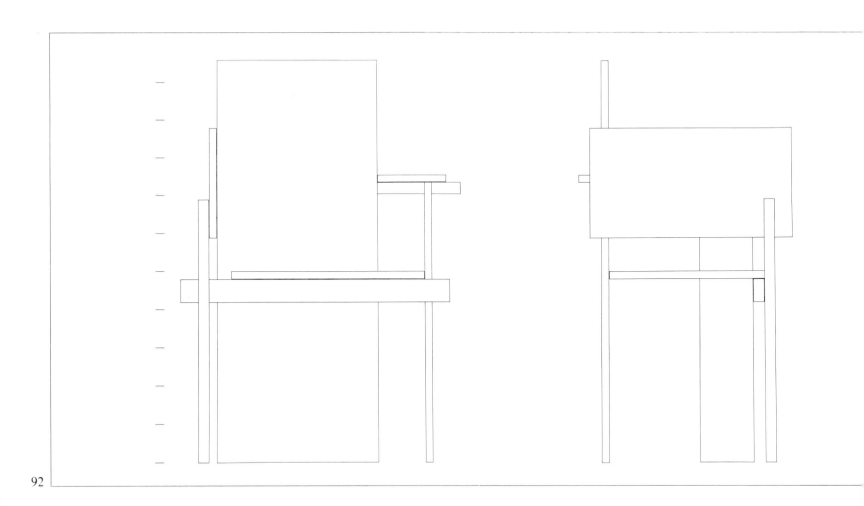

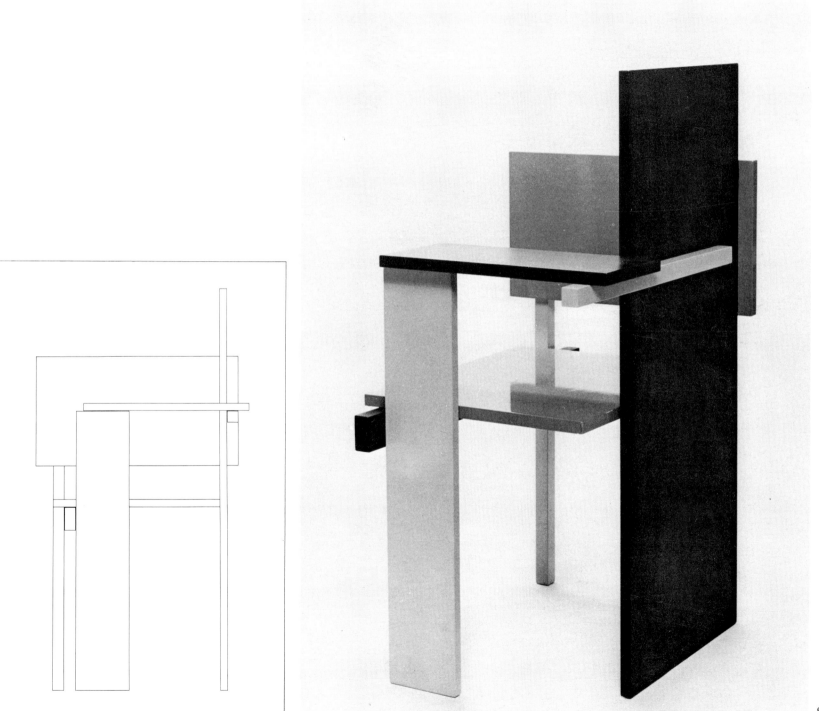

17. DIVANTAFELTJE (End table), 1923.
In deal lacquered in the colors red, blue, yellow,
black, and white. 50×50×59.5 cm.

Exh.: Utrecht, 1958; Amsterdam, 1971; London,
1972; Zürich, 1973.

Repr.: *Bouwkundig Weekblad*, 1924; *Wendingen*,
1927; T. M. Brown, 1958; P. Overy, 1969; *Cat. G.
Rietveld architect*, 1971; "Rietveld Schröder
Huis . . ." 1975.

Coll.: Amsterdam, Stedelijk Museum; Utrecht,
Schröder Huis.

*Designed and executed by Rietveld for the Schröder
Huis.*

*Design of a piece of furniture prepared by Rietveld for
the Schröder Huis bedroom area.*

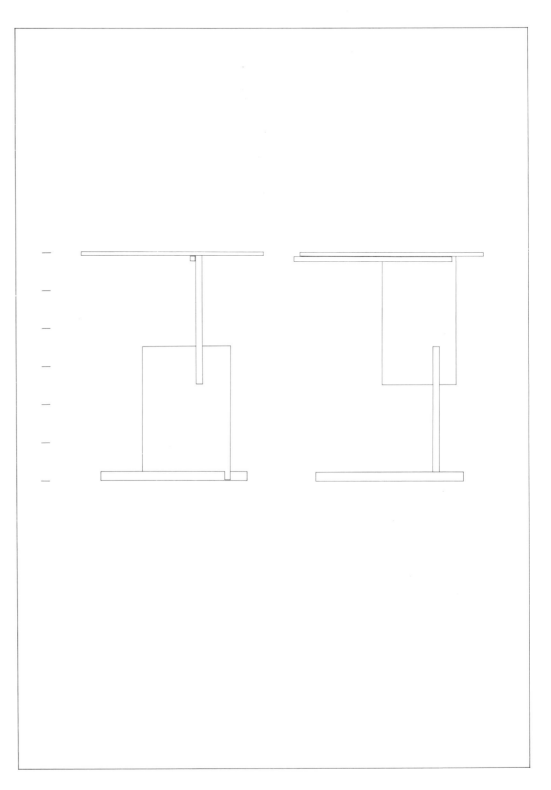

94

Schröder Huis: Rietveld's design for a corner of the living room and a photograph of it after it was constructed, published in De Stijl, *nos. 85, 86, 1928.*

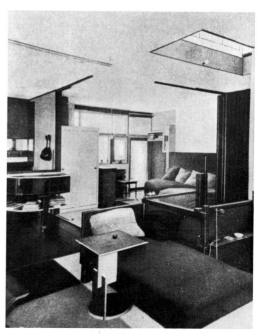

Contamination with Metal: The Use of Curved Metal Tubing in Furniture

33

34

38

39

43

44

35

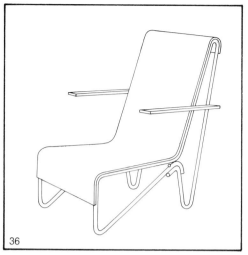

36

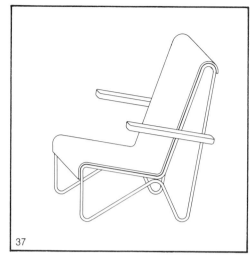

37

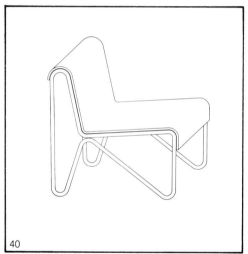

40

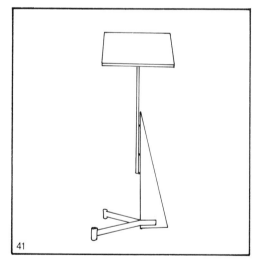

41

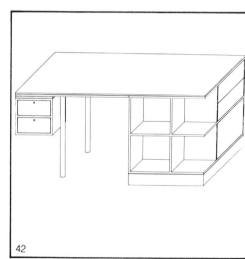

42

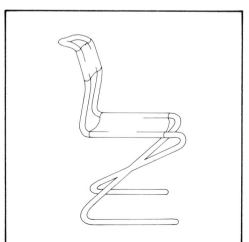

45

33. Stoel, c. 1926, metal tube and laminated wood.
34. Stoel, 1927, metal tubing with leather straps.
35. Armstoel, c. 1927, in varnished metal tubing and laminated wood.
36. Beugelfauteuil, 1927.
37. Beugelfauteuil, 1927, variant.
38. Beugelfauteuil, 1927, variant.
39. Beugelstoel, 1928.
40. Beugelstoel, 1928.
41. Muziekstandaard, 1928.
42. Bureau, 1931.
43. Fauteuil, c. 1921, in metal tubing and laminated wood.
44. Bed, 1933.
45. Buisstoel, 1933.

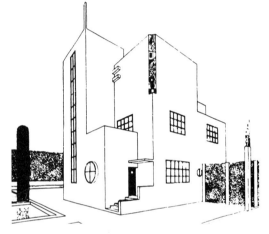

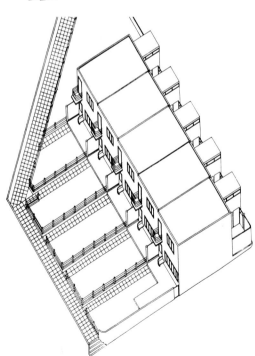

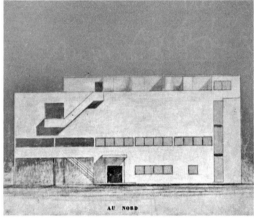

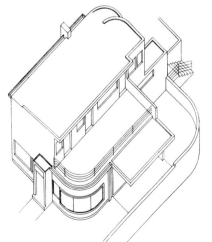

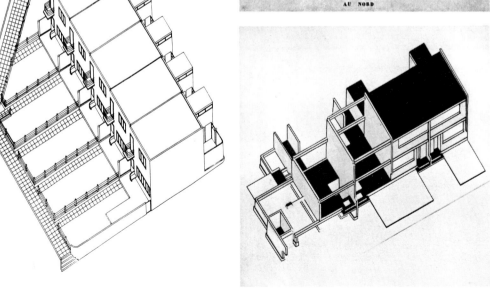

A. Loos, Steiner House, 1910.
R. Mallet-Stevens, villa, 1923.
98 *H. Scharound, house in the Weissenhof, 1927.*

L. Mies van der Rohe, villa, 1923.
M. Stam, design, 1925.
J. J. P. Oud, terraced houses at the Weissenhof, 1927.

Le Corbusier, Stein House at Garches, 1926.
W. Gropius, houses in Dessau-Törten, 1928.

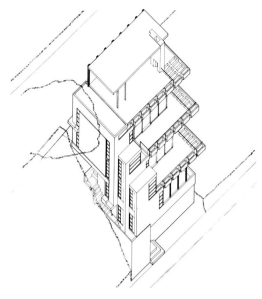

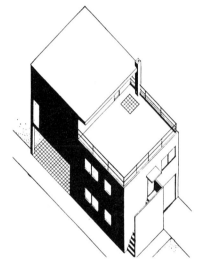

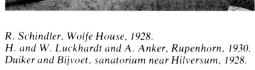

R. Schindler, Wolfe House, 1928.
H. and W. Luckhardt and A. Anker, Rupenhorn, 1930.
Duiker and Bijvoet, sanatorium near Hilversum, 1928.

A. Sartoris, design, 1927.
E. May, house in Frankfurt, c. 1930.
A. Aalto, Viipui Library, 1927-35.

G. Terragni, fascist administration, Como, 1930.
T. van Doesburg, house at Meudon Val Fleury, 1929.
G. Rietveld, Rij Huizen, Vienna, 1930-32.

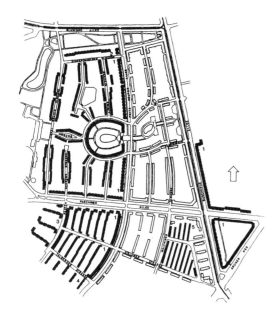

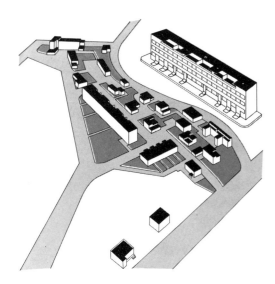

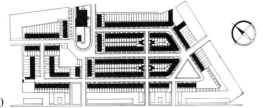

The decade which followed the end of the First World War was crowded with dramatic events. In nearly every country profound social transformations were taking place or about to take place. Inspired by the Russian Revolution other attempts at popular revolt followed, but after more than one unsuccessful revolution and the failure of the Spartacists in Germany, there occurred in all parts of Europe (and across the Atlantic also) periods of extreme social unrest, unemployment, general strikes, and insubordination by soldiers and sailors, alternating with other periods when reaction and military power held the countries in a crushing grip. At this time, German culture represented the center of gravity for international events. In Germany the Social Democrats, who were called upon to form a government with a new formula, chose Weimar as their headquarters and gave the first German republic the name of that idyllic little town, too frequently associated with the age of Goethe and Schiller, but very far in spirit from the restless proletariat of Berlin. [1]

The affirmation of liberty and democracy in Germany remained one of the great hopes of the democrats in neighboring countries as well, but the democracy of the Weimar Republic was so fragile that for fourteen years the pendulum swung between the possibility of strengthening it and abandoning it for dictatorship. With all this instability, European society passed through some transformations, though these often presented chaotic and anomalous forms. In addition, the requirements of daily life changed: housing problems no longer concerned a small elite, but extended to all the masses. As the new production faced the international market, it became conceived as production for a mass market.

Architecture tended to anticipate these social transformations by seeking to impose its new laws which inevitably produced new codes of practice: new materials, new techniques, and above all a new conception of form which led to a smaller scale of structure and an ever greater simplification.

Let us consider the period under examination, 1925–33, corresponding approximately to the building by Gropius of the new Bauhaus headquarters in Dessau and the seizure of power by the Nazis—a date which marks the end of all avant-garde experimentation in art and architecture in Germany, where it was condemned as "degenerate art" [2] and publicly vilified. Its place was taken by a massive over-organized spread of the reactionary and petit bourgeois nationalist type of counter-culture which to some extent had become current throughout Europe.

The Affirmation of the "International Style" [3]

After the development we have examined, when the early rationalist architecture replaced the concept of ornamentation by the far more significant concept of space, and after the avant-garde movements had made their exciting radical ideas widely known in the years before and after the First World War, a period of consolidation followed and there was a convergence of ideas and experimentation among many European architects who had the same cultural background, due mainly to their training at centers such as Berlin, Vienna, Zürich, and Amsterdam. The influence of such masters as Behrens, Berlage, Wagner, and Loos was apparent, as was of course the influence of Wright which was common to nearly all of them. The generation of architects of the interwar years named themselves rationalists or functionalists. But this rationalism was not a real movement, even though some of its protagonists endeavored to describe it as such. It was essentially a matter of results emerging from a contingent situation, in which a contribution was made by certain technological achievements which, when made available to the new requirements of life, were often confused with the principles of real social revolutions.

As Argan has shown, in the postwar period "all European architecture is founded on the

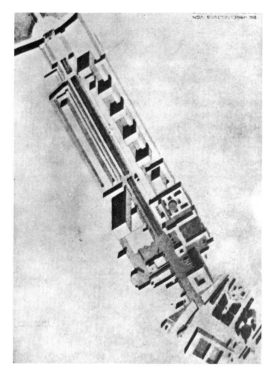

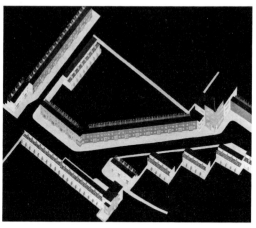

On the opposite page, from the top downward: *plan of the Berlin Britz with the buildings by B. Taut, M. Wagner, M. Taut, E. Ludwig, B. Schneidereit, 1925; the layout of the Weissenhof district buildings in Stuttgart, 1927; J. J. P. Oud, design of the Kiefhoek district, Rotterdam, 1925.*

On this page, top left: *C. van Eesteren, design for Unter den Linden, Berlin, 1925;* bottom left: *E. May, axonometry of the Frankfurt Siedlung Praunheim, 1927-30;* top right: *B. Taut, Britz district of Berlin, 1925-26;* below right: *J. J. P. Oud, Kiefhoek district, Rotterdam, 1925.*

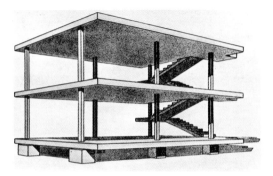

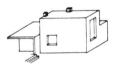

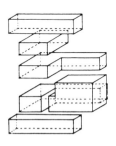

triple category of rationalism-social awareness-internationalism''[4] so amplifying the concept of the social function of art.

This time saw also the birth of the myth of reason. According to the rationalists one must believe in the renewing ethos of science which would finally put reason to the service of life. The first defeat for this idea seems to have been the expressionist irrationalism.

But the scientific approach was not uniform in the 1920s: it soon manifested itself under various tendencies, such as psychoanalysis, neopositivism, pragmatism, existentialism, and phenomenology, with the result that reason often appeared multifaceted.

In architecture there seems to have been very few clear ideas; most of them employed mystification to cover a confused language, which was new only on the surface. On the theoretical and formal plane very little that was really new emerged, at least not more than had already been said by Sant'Elia and Italian futurism, the Russian constructivists and El Lissitzky, the cubists, and, above all, De Stijl. The terms employed were vague and the linguistic instruments appeared generic. On the social plane the buildings and designs of rationalist architecture did open up vistas of hope for a different future but the language it formulated was confused, approximative, and rhetorical, and the mechanisms it set in motion were often the products of a pragmatic approach.

The concepts of the standard unit and functionalism often added up to the ideal of the machine—notoriously rhetorical in value—where the machine was taken as an aesthetic model and represented the heritage of the prewar years. Le Corbusier was the first to term rational an early-rationalist nineteenth-century type of tendency summed up in Sullivan's alliteration: ''Form follows function.''[5]

In 1931 Le Corbusier wrote to Alberto Sartoris, who asked him to write the preface to one of his books. ''The title of your work is limited and it is a pity to be forced to put the word *rational* on one side of the barricade so that the word to be written on the other side must be *academic*. In addition to *rational*, one can also say *functional*, but for me the word *architecture* contains something more magical than the rational and functional, something which dominates, predominates, imposes itself. . . .

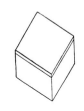

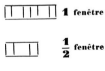

1 fenêtre

$\frac{1}{2}$ fenêtre

$\frac{1}{4}$ fenêtre

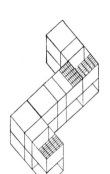

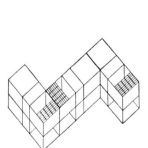

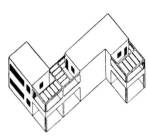

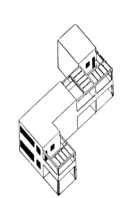

"We have barely begun. Our works are admissible for the building of a house, but for towns and social life, the foundation on which the house rests, we are only at the stage of stammering our first words. This is my intimate conviction. We owe to our theoretical or practical initiatives a far more powerful effect."[6]

Functionalism arose out of the new technology and was spurred on by its obsession with the machine, but it struggled to find a theoretical formula: reinforced concrete, glass, the new housing problems, the new scientific achievements for the benefit of the citizen and society—these were all subjects which it had to explore. But these topics were continually mixed with formal and stylistic concerns, and here the rationalist architects, even the best of them, fell into over-emphasis, revealing the limitations of the content of their theories. Sartoris began his volume in these words: "The ideas which inspire the works now being created in Europe, America, and Japan, according to the rules of geometrical and numerical splendor, a splendor made of synthesis, of noble order, of maximum precision, these are the ideas which have led modern architecture into the spheres of a golden age of renewal, of vitality surging out of the transfiguration and transposition of the utilitarian schemas of mechanical civilization. While the architects and artists of the avant-garde reaffirmed the practical concepts of the new spirit, by means of the aesthetic conquest of the machine and the incorporation of its plastic possibilities, this mechanical, organic, dynamic civilization granted contemporary architecture the faculty of entering into the time of simultaneity, into the rapid movement of space."[7] In another point in his book Sartoris continued: "Clarified by the inexorable potency of the mechanical civilization, architecture has today liberated itself to a large extent from the inert weight of symbolism and archeological old age. If the advent of the machine cuts in two the history of the plastic and figurative arts, then functionalism with its rigorously geometric formulas enhances architecture and leads it irrevocably toward pure beauty, complete form, the integral and beneficent volume. The group of scientific discoveries of the present century generates a new awareness whose factors transcend the material elements and encourage new plastic units, new architectonic vigor, aesthetic perfection, and artistic precision."[8]

The idea of contrasting the rational city as an instrument of society in progress with the monumental city representing centralized power, was certainly a utopian concept. The most utopian of all modern architects was Le Corbusier, the last heir to the illuminist tradition, who put before the world his "Ville Radieuse" which would enable all men to live in a mystical serenity, without any social barriers, in a new spirit.

Even Le Corbusier, when he considered the use of architectural materials, was unable to avoid a pantheistic exaltation and a reference to the eternal and unchangeable canons of harmony. "There now exists the architecture which is concerned with our homes, our comforts, and our feelings. Comfort and proportion. Thought and aesthetics. Machines and plasticity. Serenity and beauty."[9] However, he did attain literary sublimation in his praise of purism in the famous Law of White Lead: "If some Solon imposed these two laws on our ferment: 'the law of white lead' and 'limewash,' we would perform a moral act: To love purity!; we would increase our status: To have a measure of judgment! An act leading to the joy of living: the search for perfection.

"Think of the results of the Law of White Lead. Each citizen is compelled to remove his curtains, damasks, wallpapers, hangings, pictures made by stencil, and replace them with a pure layer of white glaze or enamel. Each person cleans his *own house*, there are no longer any dirty corners, any dark corners anywhere at all: *everything is seen just as it is.* Then he cleans up *inside himself* by entering into an order of ideas where one rejects everything which is not lawful, authorized, desired, willed, accepted: one acts only after having first thought. When shadows and dark corners are all around you, you exist in your

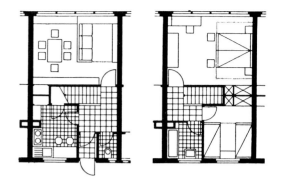

Plan of the home proposed to the 1929 CIAM in Frankfurt as a model of Existenzminimum.

On the opposite page: *Le Corbusier and P. Jeanneret, the standard* Dom-ino *skeleton structure, designed for the construction of terraced houses, 1914; W. Gropius, building parts and examples of possible combinations, c. 1928; Le Corbusier and P. Jeanneret, studies of types of building for the* Maison standardisée, *c. 1923.*

Rietveld's "Kern Huizen" (apple core) design, 1929: a prefabricated system incorporating the service block around which the dwelling develops.

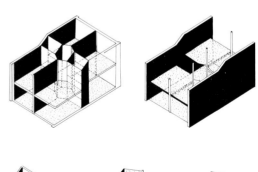

Le Corbusier, design of the living room for the Pavillon Esprit Nouveau, Paris, 1925.

G. Rietveld (with T. Schröder), interior of a show apartment in the Rij Huizen, Utrecht, 1930-31.

home only as far as the opaque limit of these corners, where your eyes cannot penetrate; you are not masters in your own home. However, with a dash of white paint on your walls, you will be *masters of yourselves*. And then you will wish to be precise; to be right, to think clearly. You will surround yourselves with order when your work has created confusion. After work you will tidy up, you will see what it has produced: you will remove what cannot be utilized and carry forward the balance to a new account. . . . The Law of White Lead would bring with it the joy of living, the joy of acting. Solon, give us at last the Law of White Lead!''[10]

Further on he continued: "Limewash has been associated with man's dwelling places ever since the birth of humanity; the stones are calcinated, ground, distempered in water, and the walls are made of a very pure white: a white which has an extraordinary beauty.

"If the house is white all over, the form of things stands out without the possibility of confusion; the volume emerges sharply; the color of objects is categorical. Limewash is absolute, everything stands out against it and is inscribed on it absolutely, black on white; it has in itself strength and loyalty. . . .

"Limewash is the wealth of the poor and the rich, the wealth of everyone, in the same way as bread, water, and milk are the wealth of both slave and king.''[11]

This infatuation with white accentuated Le Corbusier's Mediterranean view of architecture, to which he himself admitted: "I believed especially in the invincible attraction of the Mediterranean.'' [12]

We see, therefore, that the rhetoric employed in the rationalist language did not even exclude a harking back to Greek classicism and to the great eternal monuments, "the glory of the human spirit''; the discourse on beauty was revived, so directly connecting rationalism with the academic tradition.

But Le Corbusier also pointed out the theoretical insufficiency of functionalism: "Architecture supersedes utilitarian necessities. You take stone, wood, and concrete, and out of these materials you construct houses and palaces. This is what building means. The talent is in the work. But suddenly you touch my heart and fill me with joy. I am happy and say: this is beautiful. This is architecture, art has made its entry.''[13] It is here that the greatest interest arises, when the tension emerges which pushes the rationalist theories toward semantics.

Even such a man as Oud, who was always measured and reticent in his statements, allowed himself to be carried away by over-enthusiasm. He wrote in 1926: "The development which is now taking place obviously tends toward an architecture which is more than ever connected in its essence to materials, but in its outer appearance it will show that it can surpass them. This architecture, freed from any impressionistic state of mind, will arrive in full light of day at a purity of relationships, a flash of colors and an organic clarity of forms which, lacking any accessory element, will be able to surpass the purity of classicism.''[14]

When matter was discussed it was in relation to its dependence upon form; and it was in form that matter could reveal its qualities, but here we are in an illusory field, where a dominant materiality was meant to emphasize the purity of forms.

Only Mies van der Rohe, with his German pavilion in the 1929 Barcelona exhibition, succeeded in rendering the construction immaterial by means of an illusory architecture. He transformed walls and marble slabs into abstract planes and opened up new horizons for the followers of Rietveld's Schröder Huis. It was a symbolic work where the concept of functionalism could be so expanded as to become unrecognizable when compared with the schemes formulated up to that time. Possibly no one has described this more incisively than Zevi: "With the German pavilion in Barcelona of 1929 and the model house in the 1931 Berlin exhibition, the volumetric style of neoplasticism is resolved in a spatial key.

G. Rietveld (with T. Schröder), the Rij Huizen, Utrecht; below: *in* Erasmuslaan, *nos. 5-11, 1931;* bottom: *in* Erasmuslaan *and* Prins Hendriklaan, *1934.*

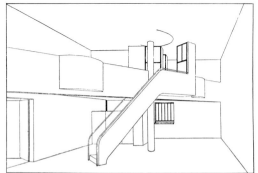

Le Corbusier, Villa Savoye, Poissy, 1929-30, interior; Maison en série pour artisans, 1924, interior; G. Rietveld, interior of the Hondius-Crone building at Vijverhof, Bloemendaal, 1935.

"Unlike Van Doesburg and Rietveld, Mies does not need to take a box-shaped building as his starting point, disconnecting its corners, differentiating its walls and cutting them up into more or less juxtaposed rectangles in various colors—a task which is fundamentally skin-deep and leaves the spatial rhythm unaltered. For Mies the box does not exist: Wright destroyed it, so that it is useless to make an effort to dismember it. He starts off with a continuous space, uninterrupted between exterior and interior, and in no case ensnared within four walls, and he channels its currents through partitions, which by being prolonged beyond the slabs of the floor and roof, establish an unceasing dialogue between the open building and the surrounding area."[15]

This was the culminating moment in a complex and tortuous historical period and was soon to make way for new orientations and new tendencies.

A less rhetorical movement which came closer to the needs of daily life was represented by the investigation into the conditions of urban living, leading to a radical change in building in Germany around 1925. This was assisted by the solid presence of the Deutscher Werkbund which kept the discussion going and presented its results in regular exhibitions and also by the enlightened attitude of certain local administrations.

An exceptional undertaking was the reconstruction of the city of Frankfurt, entrusted to Ernst May (1925–31),[16] and an imposing task was the construction of the Britz in Berlin (1925), mainly the work of Bruno Taut. Many rationalists took as an example the Stuttgart Weissenhof, which was coordinated by Mies van der Rohe on the occasion of an exhibition of the Werkbund in 1927. Finally, a notable example of prefabricated building was the Dessau-Torten district by Gropius (1926–28). In Germany in 1928 a national institute for economic research into residential building was set up[17] which rationalized resources and the means available for the construction of the districts of Frankfurt, Stuttgart, and Dessau just mentioned.

These developments laid the foundations for the setting up of the CIAM,[18] a series of international congresses at which the best-known architects were to participate as delegates of their nations. The first congress was held in the Castle of La Sarraz (Switzerland) in 1928, and the second in Frankfurt in 1929. The latter was much less generic in its content and discussed the *Existenzminimum*, a debate which aroused questions of a moral as well as social nature and encouraged many of the participants to devote themselves more wholeheartedly to the problem of housing the poorest sectors of society. Gropius wrote concerning this: "The question of the minimum house is the question of the basic minimum of space, air, light, and heat which is necessary to man. . . . Man from a biological viewpoint needs improved conditions of ventilation and lighting and only a small quantity of living space, especially if this is organized in a technically correct manner."[19]

The time of the first CIAM congresses is without doubt the time when the ideas of the internationalist movement were most closely allied and it is also the time when questions of form seemed to take second place. The use of a simpler style turns the interest toward a heightened spatial tension, circumscribing the Ration Wohnung, the *quantum* essential to man's basic existence.

Form and Function

The Swiss Adolf Behne wrote in 1923: "Nothing is more comprehensible than the fact that the rationalist should place particular emphasis on form: this is born when human relations are instituted. The single individual, isolated in the midst of nature, is free. The problem of form arises at the same time as that of the union of several individuals, in fact form is the conditions which makes living together possible. Form is an eminently social factor. Anyone who accepts the laws of society also accepts those of form."[20]

As we have seen, the spatial-volumetric conception of the rationalists, unlike that of De Stijl, is similar to the neoclassical conception and is expressed through the medium of simple solids (the solids of Philebus) especially the cube and parallelepiped. But can these elements suffice to create absolute forms which must still be dependent upon precise functions? The problem of codification arises also. Indeed, is it possible to codify such functions? Umberto Eco in a work on architecture and semiology[21] has provided some very important indications for an understanding of the relationship between form and function: "That which architecture puts into form (a system of social relationships, a way of living and being together) does not belong to architecture since it could be defined and named even if by hypothesis architecture did not exist. . . . The system of functions does not belong to the language of architecture, but in fact stands outside it."[22]

And the following statement of his seems to contain the essential point: "All mystiques of 'form following function' remain mystiques and nothing else unles they rest on a consideration of plans for codification. In communicative terms, the principle that form follows function signifies that the form of the object must not only make the function possible, but must denote it so clearly as to make it desirable as well as practicable, and turn to the movements most capable of fulfilling it."[23]

The architecture of rationalism is founded on the dichotomy of *form* (or geometry) and *function*. We know that the rationalists aspired to reach an absolute, pure, and essential form which would exist outside of history.

"A form which is imponderable and rarefied, purged of all sentimental or emotional content, immune from any residue of nature, unattackable as a concept and, like every conceptual truth, without limit and repeatable to infinity; a form which is not in space, but

G. Rietveld, Huis en muziekschool, Zeist, 1932.   107

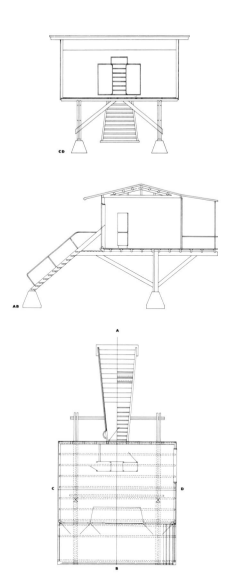

G. Rietveld (with T. Schröder), Week-end Huis, small house measuring 7.4 m. in diameter, with six bed places, presented at the Utrecht Fair, 1938.

is space itself, a continuous 'movement through space'; a structure woven by men themselves with their rational actions, and both a condition and expression of that rationalism in progress; this is the supreme ideal of the new aesthetics, which rejects even this name and wishes to be nothing more than a theory of formativity, a *Gestaltungstheorie*."[24]

But in actual fact, in spite of its claims to be scientific and unswervingly loyal to the new technologies, rationalist architecture was anchored in the theory of empiricism and this is the reason for the vagueness of its language and the uncertainty of its conclusions.

Rietveld the Architect

What place did Rietveld hold in the general architectural discussion of the 1930s? After building the Schröder Huis, Rietveld was now an established architect, at least in the circle of the profession, both in the Netherlands and elsewhere. The last editions of *De Stijl* appeared in 1927 (if we exclude the two anniversary numbers celebrating the tenth birthday of the journal in 1928 and the special issue of 1932). Many of its founders and supporters had by now left the group. Oud and Rietveld were considered the only architects who could properly represent the defunct movement. Rietveld was very interested in developments in Europe during this period and wished to play a greater part on the international scene. Together with Oud, Van Eesteren, and Stam, he was a Dutch delegate at the founding of the CIAM in 1928. He accepted the rationalist trend, adopted the concept of Zakelijkheid,[25] and joined in the debate on the *Existenzminimum* at the Frankfurt CIAM.

He was now too much alone to pursue an avant-garde policy which appeared excessively utopian to most people. In addition, he could not afford to neglect market trends. For his part Oud had long ago chosen a more moderate path, not accepting—and sometimes rejecting outright—some of the manifestations of De Stijl. He had long ago made his way of thinking into his program, which can be identified in the following extract: "To sum up, one can arrive at this conclusion, that an architecture which is founded rationally on the conditions of today will from all points of view conflict with architecture as it has been until today. Without falling into an arid rationalism, it will be based essentially on reality, but in this meaning of reality it will immediately be able to experience the most noble sentiments."[26]

According to Rietveld, "Functional architecture must not confine itself to meeting the necessities of life; it must also create conditions of life; it must not simply establish space; it must experience it intensely. . . . It is to this end that we can apply new possibilities of construction and new materials. They help clearly to define the designated spaces."[27]

One of his most interesting buildings in this period was the house with garage for a caretaker-chauffeur (1927) built out of prefabricated cement blocks joined together by painted steel corners. Once again Rietveld showed himself an innovator, being one of the first architects to work in the field of prefabrication. In 1928 he rebuilt the Zaudy store in Wesel, Germany. Working on a façade built entirely in glass, he set a cube-shaped shop window in front of it to jut out diagonally, forming a great contrast with the traditional two-dimensional fronts of the surrounding houses. But his most interesting projects were associated with the building of homes for ordinary people. He found the problems of minimal dwelling congenial and faced them with great enthusiasm. The *Kern Huizen* ("apple core") project begun in 1928 consisted of a prefabricated nucleus with a hexagonal ground plan containing the service areas, water and electricity installations, around which the other areas gravitated.

The Utrecht "Rij Huizen," 1930–31

Following the same direction as he had taken in 1928 with the Kern Huizen, Rietveld designed these inexpensive homes for the working class by grouping the service areas and stairs in a vertical direction. On the ground floor he placed the kitchen-living room-breakfast room; above on two levels were the bedrooms. Small gardens adjoined the ground floor area.

The materials used were a combination of bricks and steel with wide glass panels. This arrangement produced an ideally lit working area—the light was so well distributed through the space that the contrast between light and shadow was automatically lessened, thus eliminating the need for the eye to adapt itself to variable intensities of light. The same system was later used in industrial and school buildings.

Also in 1931 Rietveld was asked to design houses for the Wiener Werkbund-siedlung in Vienna. Again in these low-income homes the problem was to work on a minimum amount of space. The base area of each unit was only 4/8 m. The rooms, on different levels, were connected by a spiral staircase.

In 1934 he designed four Rij Huizen in Utrecht, close to those built in 1930–31.

Of especial interest is the diagonal plan: the internal space was organized in such a way that each family occupied a living area placed above a lower living area with which it was interconnected diagonally. As in his earlier works, the breakfast room and living room could be separated by means of sliding partitions.

While adhering to functionalism and constructing in masses of a rigorous stereometry, with rationalized arrangement and repetitions of the individual elements, Rietveld always operated with a neoplastic conception of architecture which differentiated him considerably from the more manneristic style of rationalism.

In 1933 he made for the firm Metz & Company, with whom he had been collaborating since 1930, a panoramic exhibition pavilion at the top of a late baroque nineteenth-century building. From this circular platform a view could be obtained of the objects exhibited in a context broader than the pavilion itself, with a panoramic view over the whole city of Amsterdam.

But apart from his work as an architect and the making of a few articles of furniture, one of the most surprising features of those years was the interest Rietveld manifested in theoretical problems connected with optics, even though the ideas he expressed did not reveal any new concepts. Just when other architects were pronouncing on the future of architecture, frequently in a mannered way and in excessively literary terms, Rietveld drew up a series of *Inzicht*[28] which reveal a most detailed and careful study of the psychology of sight and demonstrate his feeling for a correct and methodical way of working in the world of form and time-space.

This readiness to enter into the cultural debate at an international level, and his immediate recognition of the themes which count in developing a constructive and nonempirical dialogue, finally give the lie to the figure of Rietveld as nothing more than a craftsman who seized on ideas thought out and developed by others.

To try to discover where truth lies he adopted the same process of analytical de-composition with which he had long been familiar in De Stijl: as in architecture, he analyzed and broke up everything until he reached its essential nucleus, and from there he started off to construct his mental plan.

Concerning prefabrication and units of measure, for example, he wrote: "Because I am an ardent supporter of prefabrication, I keep looking for units of measure which will be suitable for universal adoption. Apart from practical considerations, in each specific object I seek the ideal measure, the maximum unit of measure possible which would

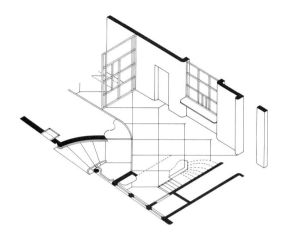

G. Rietveld, *layout of the entrance to the Hypothecair Crediet bank in Carel van Bylandlaan, The Hague, 1939-40.*

G. Rietveld, *Zaudy shop, Wesel, 1928.*

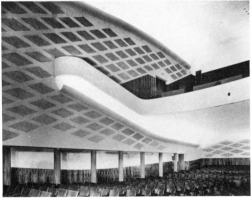

G. Rietveld (with T. Schröder), cinema-theater
Vreeburg, Utrecht, 1936.

clearly reveal the proportions of the building. As in a cinema film, our eye is able to capture thousands of details in a single instant, but is limited in range so that it can grasp only a few elements with a single glance. Generally speaking, objects or buildings which contain only a small number of principal elements represent the most impeccable units. A proper distribution of measurements in a building creates a crystalline clarity which can be called, with good reason, one of the secrets of a good work of architecture."[29]

In his *Inzicht* he emphasized the retina's attempt to single out objects and its behavior when confronted with any kind of object: "All we experience is founded on our senses of observation. . . . Color for example, which we note directly by 'perceiving it,' we measure by means of mercury. But while color is barely perceptible according to our senses, science measures it by means of waves and angles of incidence. . . . Our method of seeing is distinguished into the categories of: sense of color, sense of form, and sense of space. If we see a three-dimensional form, our retina acts on the various distances, following the form and material of the object. . . . By sense of space one must understand a certain position of the retina in relation to the lens. The more senses there are working simultaneously, the less intensive will be the observation of reality. . . . The direct experience of the competent senses is the stabilization and growth of our being."[30] When submitted to formal analysis, his architecture is therefore a direct consequence of the theory of art evolved by Fiedler which no longer declares itself a theory of the beautiful, but a theory of "pure visibility," taken to the extreme consequences from where, through the mastery of the laws of optics, a correct perception of the work can be attained.

Furniture Made of Curved Metal Tubing

"And when a movement ends or flows into another, it still remains a living parcel of our consciousness. No single country, no one person, has created our furniture or the equipment of the house. Each land contributed its atmosphere, its talents, whenever an idea was being worked out. This co-operation guarantees the validity of the whole development.

"No sooner has a new idea appeared—the tubular chair for instance—than its implications are worked out by new creative talents, only to return to the inventor who resolves them into standard form."[31]

This passage by Giedion seems to express very well the complexity of the situation which came into being after De Stijl. Giedion himself, who described Rietveld's furniture (of the period 1918–24 to be precise) as manifestos, said of rationalist furniture that "around 1925 the transposition from the manifesto to the standard product took place. With disturbing rapidity distribution began."[32]

The history of design reflects the history of architecture and each of their phases coincides. The metal tube chair represents the same spatial intentions and the same striving for technological renewal that were seen in the large works of architecture produced during those years. And the impulse to create these chairs derived from the desire to obtain a light and spatial structure, almost as if suspended in the air. In the Bauhaus furniture workshop around the year 1925 designers were engaged on types which were entirely different from those of the artisan tradition and technique, partly because they were influenced by the needs of industry. Marcel Breuer constructed his first armchair out of Mannesman unwelded tubes in that year with the help of some of the students in his course.

"The exact stages leading to an invention cannot be reconstructed. The glistening handle bars of a bicycle may have led Marcel Breuer to use the same material for chairs. The tubular steel chair may perhaps have links with the earlier bent-wood chair" of curved wood by Thonet which had been widely distributed in Europe and America for many decades.[33] But there is one thing which cannot be overlooked: "In this case the material itself, the metal tube, is already an industrial product. Since one cannot conceive of an intricate process actuated through the intervention of an artisan technique upon a material produced industrially, the only expressive process which can now be admitted by this type of conception is that of industrial production."[34]

A further evolution in the form taken by this object occurred around 1926–27. In one of the terraced houses built at the Stuttgart Weissenhof, the house built by the Dutch architect Martin Stam to be precise, there were two metal tube chairs of the type of those designed by Breuer, but without any backrest; the chair ended on the floor and the seat was not supported by a steel tube: this was the first example of a protruding or sloping chair.

The first model of these chairs was made in a very rudimentary fashion by Martin Stam, with gas tubing held together by corner joints, in about the previous year.[35] Stam's chair was followed, again in Stuttgart, by the far more elegant chair of Mies van der Rohe, who was often consulted by Stam. In this form Mies obtained the greatest elasticity which derived from the suppleness of the tubular structure.

A final version of this chair form was later produced by Breuer who in 1928 put it into the hands of the Thonet workshop for production in the form in which it reaches us today.

In 1928 Le Corbusier, together with Pierre Jeanneret and Charlotte Periand, produced the famous series of large and small armchairs—chaise longue, confort et grand confort, siège à dossier basculant—but even before that, in 1925, he became engrossed in problems of decor. He exhibited his Pavillon de l'Esprit Nouveau at the Exposition des Arts Décoratifs in Paris (in collaboration with Jeanneret) and published the volume L'art décoratif d'aujourd'hui,[36] a deliberately polemical title intended to draw attention to the retrograde view of industrial design held by the French. This was Le Corbusier's opportunity to demolish many taboos and commonplace ideas and to show his own readiness to pursue new directions: "We must first state unequivocally that there is no reason why wood should remain the prime material of furniture. If it is asked to do so, industry is ready to offer many new things: steel, aluminium, cement (given special treatment), fibers, and . . . what we do not yet know about! . . . In the manufacture of airplanes and car bodies wood is used in such a new way that the wooden article of furniture no longer has the right to be thought of as it once was, and we—you and I—who hold a view of 'furniture' which conforms to our traditional outlook, we find we have become unserviceable: we all have to start reeducating ourselves."[37]

But the chairs, armchairs, and tables designed by Le Corbusier arose out of a different initial conception and in their relationship between form and signified element the connotations appear more complex. From a visual viewpoint the structural signs (or syntactic codes) were superseded by the cultural and semantic, belonging to both an international and a national culture at the same time, where—as was the case with another French designer of the period, Eileen Gray—a vaguely Art Deco influence persisted.

But the model furniture which had now become current throughout the world and which more than any other represented the rationalist theory, was that produced in Dessau: it exemplified technology and new materials, lightness and transparency, functionalism and the possibility of mass production. In Törten near Dessau 316 minimal dwellings were completed in 1928 to a design by Gropius. Most of the furniture for these homes came from the Bauhaus workshops, which in this way began a semi-industrial type of production. Even the distribution of the objects within space, the type of layout proposed by Gropius and Breuer, which was added to what had previously been envisaged for the

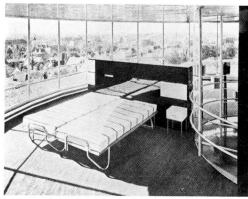

G. Rietveld, Metz & Co., exhibition pavilion; circular platform at the top of the baroque building in Leidschestraat, Amsterdam, with a panoramic view over the city, 1933; below: design of a shop window with a new logotype pattern.

Armchair no. 9 of the Thonet series, called the Wiener Stuhl, and selected by Le Corbusier for the Pavillon l'Esprit Nouveau.

teachers' apartments in Dessau, was imposed as a logical solution, a spatial entity transmuted into dogma.

For his part, Rietveld turned to rational furniture after 1926 for two precise reasons: because he was in contact with some of the protagonists of the new trend, such as Martin Stam—and this could not have failed to stimulate him to experiment technologically with metal tubing—and for reasons of public demand. In fact, he had to provide samples of decor for the new buildings constructed by himself which, as we have seen, had now become part of the International Style.

The first object of some importance which he completed was a small armchair with a support made of fiber to serve as a combined backrest and seat, and supported on the two sides by a surrounding tubular structure where the metal tube took the form of an added circular structure. The two arms were added in relief.

From the viewpoint of its connotative significance this chair bears no comparison with those by Mies and Le Corbusier, nor does it represent an innovation on the technological plane as did Breuer's and Stam's. But Rietveld was not an imitator of anyone and did not give up following his own path, with the result that this armchair too has its personal identity which imposes itself on the viewer. He later changed the dimensions of the armchair and produced some variants without arms. By the irony of fate it was these metal articles, which he designed because of his association with the international movement, which brought him the first mass production in his life, when they were taken up in 1930 by the Dutch firm Metz & Company.

For some years Rietveld continued to experiment with new forms of furniture employing this technique and just before he returned to the use of wood he concluded this cycle with a chair which may well be considered the most interesting object of this period. This was the ''Buisstoel,'' made in 1933. As before in Stam's chair, a single steel tube outlines the structure of the seat, joined below the seat in the form of an X and concluding in two legs to give it stability; the seat and back are made of stretched cloth. Many have seen in this seat the metal version of the ''Zigzag,'' shown to the public the following year; but this view is not correct since it ignores Rietveld's research into the material and its properties which was resolved in the material through which he imprinted on the chair an unmistakable connotative value.

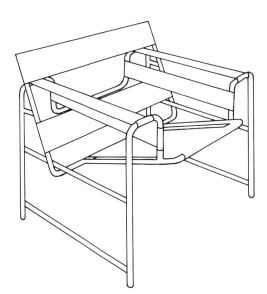

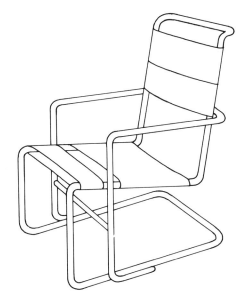

The most significant armchairs employing curved metal tubing.
M. Breuer, 1925.
M. Stam, 1925-26.
L. Mies van der Rohe, 1927.
V. Tatlin, 1927.
Le Corbusier, 1928.

[1] For a social and political study of the Weimar Republic and its relations with art and architecture in Germany, see the essay by Enzo Collotti, in *Controspazio*, 4–5 (April–May 1970), an issue entirely devoted to the Bauhaus.

[2] On this problem, see Hildegard Bremer, *Die Kunstpolitik des Nationalsozialismus* (Hamburg, 1963).

[3] A definition arrived at by Henry Russell Hitchcock and Philip Johnson, *The International Style: Architecture since 1922* (New York, 1932). They were the first to apply this term to the architecture of the 1920s and 1930s.

[4] Giulio Carlo Argan, *Gropius e la Bauhaus*.

[5] Reyner Banham, *Theory and Design in the First Machine Age*.

[6] Alberto Sartoris, *Elementi dell'Architettura funzionale* (Milan, 1932).

[7] Ibid.

[8] Ibid.

[9] Le Corbusier, *L'art décoratif d'aujourd'hui* (Paris, 1925).

[10] Ibid.

[11] Ibid.

[12] Ibid.

[13] Le Corbusier, *Vers une architecture* (Paris, 1926).

[14] J.J.P. Oud, *Holländische Architektur* (Bauhausbücher: Munich, 1926).

[15] Bruno Zevi, *Poetica dell'architettura neoplastica*, rev. ed. (Turin, 1974). In the 1st ed. (Milan, 1953), this extract is worded slightly differently but its meaning is substantially unaltered.

[16] Ernst May, "Cinque anni di attività edilizia residenziale a Francoforte," in *Controspazio*. In the same number see also Franco Borsi, "L'esperienza delle città tedesche."

[17] *Reichsforschungsgesellschaft für Wirtschaftlichkeit in Bau- und Wohnungswesen*. Martin Steinmann, "Il secondo CIAM e il problema del *Minimum*. Organizzazione dell'alloggio e Taylorismo" in *Psicon* 2-3 (January-June 1975).

[18] Congrès Internationaux de l'Architecture Moderne.

[19] Walter Gropius, *Die Soziologischen Grundlagen der Minimalwohnung* in *Die Wohnung für das Existenzminimum*, 3rd ed. (Stuttgart, 1933). Martin Steinmann, op. cit.

[20] Adolf Behne, "Der Moderne Zweckbau" (1923), in *Architettura Razionale* (Milan, 1973).

[21] Umberto Eco, *La Struttura assente*.

[22] Ibid.

[23] Ibid.

[24] Giulio Carlo Argan, *Gropius e la Bauhaus*.

[25] From the German *Sachlichkeit*, which means objectivity, concreteness, realism; understood here as an adherence to reality, to function. This was one of the terms which was put forward during the international discussions of the CIAM.

[26] J.J.P. Oud, *Holländische Architektur*.

[27] Gerrit Rietveld, "Inzicht," in *i, 10* (1928).

[28] From the English word *insight*, used by the Gestalt psychologists (in particular Köhler) in the sense of interior vision and psychological penetration.

[29] Quoted in the catalogue for *G. Rietveld architect*, Stedelijk Museum (Amsterdam, 1971).

[30] Published in *i, 10*.

[31] Siegfried Giedion, *Mechanization Takes Command*.

[32] Ibid.

[33] Ibid.

[34] Giulio Carlo Argan, *Walter Gropius e la Bauhaus*.

[35] Reyner Banham, op. cit. Banham's belief that this occurred in 1924 has not been confirmed or proved.

[36] Paris 1925. This collection of essays had previously appeared in the journal *L'Esprit Nouveau*.

[37] Ibid.

M. Stam, seat made of metal tubing and fabric, 1926; this is probably the first example of a chair in relief.

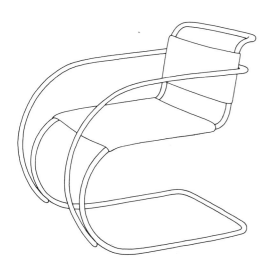

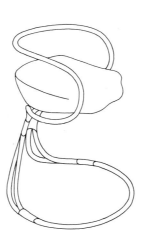

18. BEUGELFAUTEUIL (Armchair), 1927.
Made of chrome metal tubing with a diameter of 18
mm.; seat of curved plywood lacquered white or
black; 60×85×94 cm.

Exh.: Utrecht, 1958; Amsterdam, 1971; London,
1972; Amsterdam, 1975.

Repr.: J. de Jong, 1929; "Werk-Jaarboek van . . ."
1931; G. A. Platz, 1933; T. M. Brown, 1958; *Cat. G.
Rietveld architect*, 1971; H. de Jong, 1974; "Metalen
Buisstoelen . . ." 1975.

Coll.: Amsterdam, Stedelijk Museum.

*The prototype of this armchair was of larger
dimensions and the metal tube forming the structure of
the two sides was interrupted at the lower part, at the
point where it rested on the seat; the two tube sections
were welded to each other.*
*In 1930 this armchair and the two presented in the
following pages were put into production by Metz &
Co. (Amsterdam, The Hague). A variant without the
two arms was also made.*

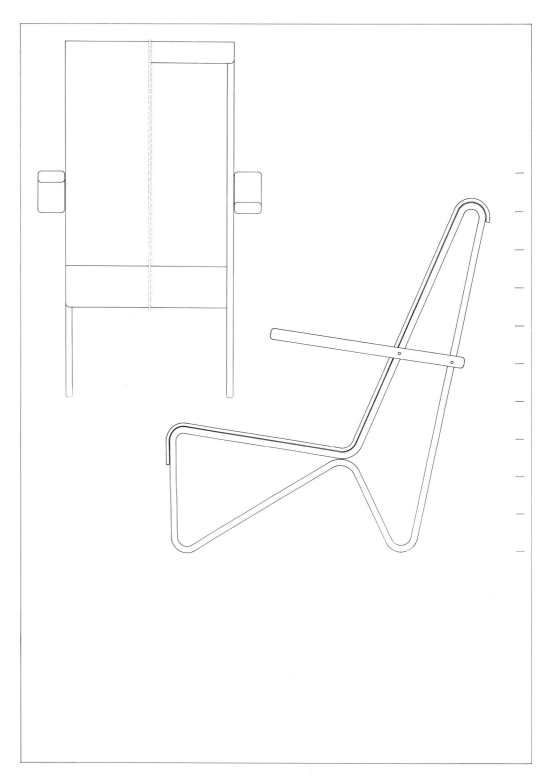

Sketches of the tubing and photo (below) *published in* De Nieuwe Richting in de Kunstnijverheid in Nederland, *Rotterdam, 1929.*

115

19. BEUGELSTOEL (Chair on tubular steel frame),
c. 1928.
Made of chrome metal tubing with a diameter of 18
mm; seat of curved plywood, lacquered in the colors
red, blue, yellow, white, or black; 40×53×73 cm.

Exh.: Utrecht, 1958; Amsterdam, 1971; London,
1972; Amsterdam, 1975.

Repr.: *Cat. G. Rietveld architect*, 1971; ''Metalen
Buisstoelen . . .'' 1975.

Coll.: Amsterdam, Stedelijk Museum.

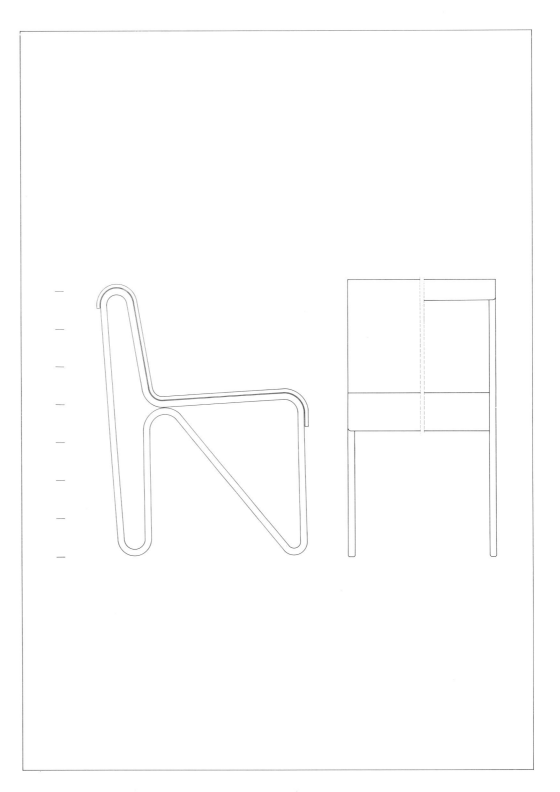

20.   BEUGELSTOEL (Chair on tubular steel frame),
c. 1928.
Made of chrome metal tubing with a diameter of 18
mm.; seat of curved plywood, lacquered in the colors
red, blue, yellow, white, or black; 40×58×60 cm.

Exh.:   Utrecht, 1958; Amsterdam, 1971; London,
1972; Amsterdam, 1975.

Repr.:   ''Metalen Buisstoelen . . .'' 1975.

Coll.:   Amsterdam, Stedelijk Museum.

This seat, like the two previously described armchairs,
was often used by Rietveld in the furnishing of the
houses he designed throughout the decade 1930-40.

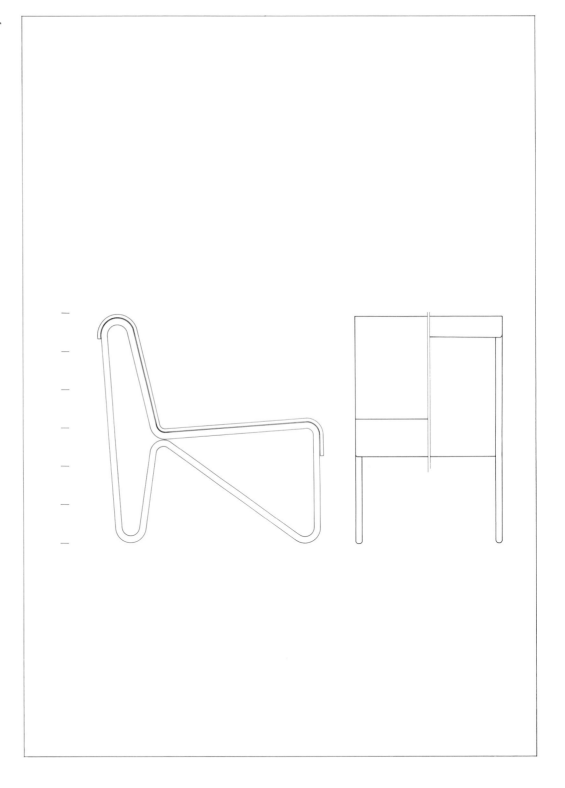

Stoel, 1927, made of steel tubing with leather thongs.

21. BUREAU (Desk), 1931.
The drawer section made of black lacquered wood
with edges and surface lacquered white; table with
supporting structure made of aluminum, surface of
black lacquered wood; table drawers black lacquered
with white edges; glass top placed over both parts of
the desk; 150×90×71 cm. (overall dimensions).

Exh.:   Amsterdam, 1971; London, 1972.

Repr.:   B. Merkelbach, 1932; T. M. Brown, 1958;
Cat. G. Rietveld architect, 1971.

Coll.:   Amsterdam, Stedelijk Museum.

*Designed in collaboration with Truus
Schröder-Schräder, the desk was put into the* Rij
Huizen *show apartment in Erasmuslaan, Utrecht, in
the same year.*

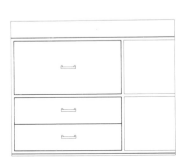

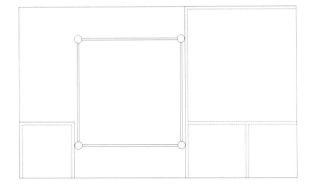

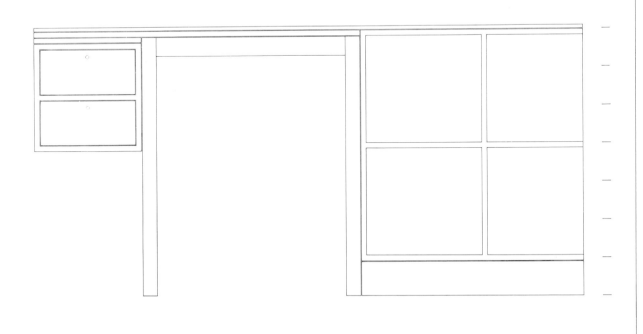

Fauteuil, c. 1931, made of curved metal tubing and laminated wood. Production Metz & Co., Amsterdam; layout by Willem Penaat; below: sketches and annotations by Rietveld relating to this desk.

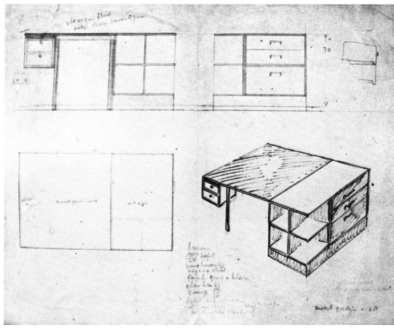

22.   BUISSTOEL (Tubular chair), 1933.
Made of curved chrome metal, with the seat and back
of fabric; 40×45×83.5 cm.

Exh.:   Amsterdam, 1975.

Repr.:   I. Falkenberg-Liefrink, 1934; T. M. Brown,
1958; *Cat. G. Rietveld architect*, 1971; ``Metalen
Buisstoelen . . .'' 1975.

Coll.:   Delft, Tj. Deelstra.

*Constructed out of a single length of tubing 4 meters
approx. in length.*
*Put into production for a short time by Metz & Co., but
certain difficulties were encountered over the choice
and curving of the material: if the tube was soft, the
seat produced a sensation of instability; if the diameter
of the tube was increased, breaks could occur at the
points where it curved. Today such difficulties would be
easily overcome. Many people consider this chair to be
a variant of the more famous ``Zigzag,'' but the
underlying conception is of quite another nature. I
consider it the last of the variations on the theme of the
chair designed by Breuer in 1925.*

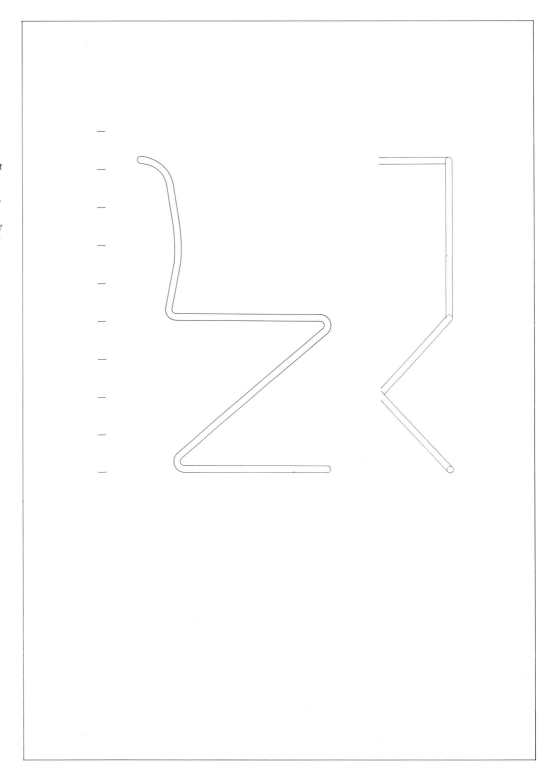

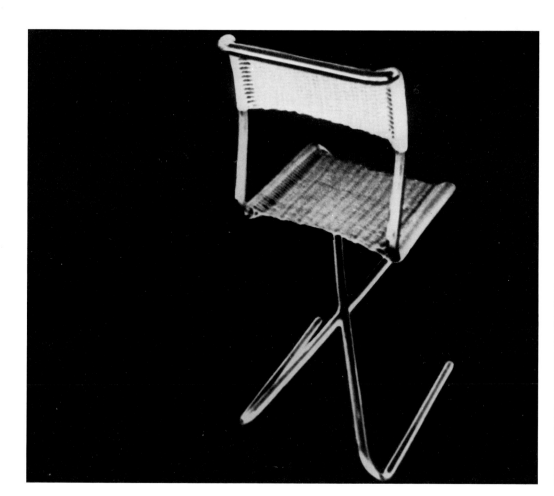

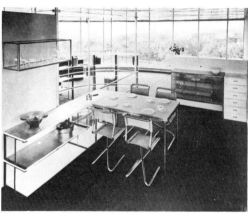

*The Buisstoelen in a decor by Metz & Co.,
Amsterdam.*

The Single-Sheet Chair

46. *Birza-fauteuil, modelled out of a single sheet of fiber.*
47. *Stoel, 1927, modelled out of a single sheet of fiber.*
48. *Stoel van gebogen triplex, c. 1930.*
49. *Aluminum fauteuil, 1942.*

46

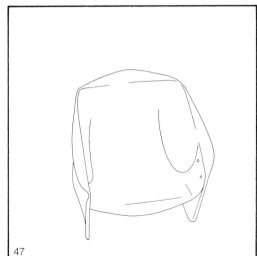

47

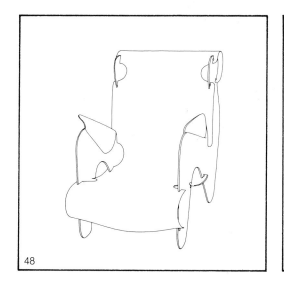

48

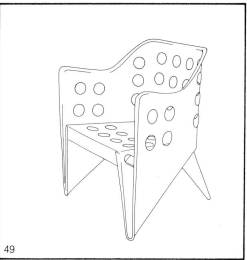

49

125

Parallel with his first experiments in chairs constructed with metal tubing, in 1927 Rietveld examined the possibility of making chairs out of a single sheet of material which would be complete in itself and incorporate no other supporting elements. It was the curved combined seat and chair back of his first metal chair which suggested this possibility to him. In fact the two designs he made in that year by this method were based on a stiffening of the material through the medium of the curve. "I have always believed that a chair ought to be no more complicated than a drawing pin,"[1] he said many years later, and this was the view on which he based his experiments. The idea of making a chair out of a single sheet formed under pressure on a suitable material was the equivalent of building a house around a central unit enclosing the service areas (kitchen, bathroom, stairs) and was closely associated with the trend toward industrialization.

Here Rietveld the designer tackled the problem by means of the single possibility which the physical properties of the material permitted him: he had before him a sheet (whether of fiber or aluminum) and intervened only at those points which were to transform it into a chair with all the characteristics denoted by this term. The achievement was both technical and psychological. All the cultural stratifications emerging from his earlier furniture no longer seemed to belong to him: De Stijl seemed forgotten. But in fact this was merely a variation on his perpetual theme: to build in terms of simplicity and intelligence, which is also a way of understanding life. Perhaps still unconsciously he was at the start of a new trend which showed itself in him and others during the next few years: the movement from rationalism to the organic tendency had begun.

[1] From an interview filmed by Piet van Monk, 1963.

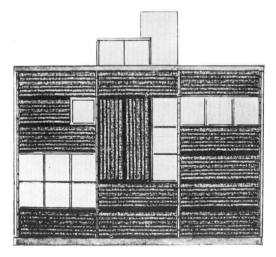

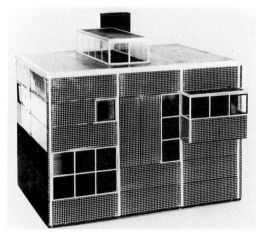

G. Rietveld, garage and house for a chauffeur in Waldeck Pyrmontkade, Utrecht, 1927, made out of prefabricated cement blocks and corner sections of painted steel; above: the design as published in De Stijl, nos. 79-84, 1927; the model; on the right: the building soon after its construction.

127

23.   ARMSTOEL VAN GEBOGEN TRIPLEX
(Armchair of laminated wood), *c.* 1930.
Made of natural deal layers with sides lacquered red;
60×94×82 cm.

Exh.:   Amsterdam, 1971; London, 1972.

Repr.:   *Cat. G. Rietveld architect*, 1971.

Coll.:   Amsterdam, Stedelijk Museum.

*The armchair is composed of three molded parts: the
two sides and the curved panel which acts as a
combined seat and back. It is assembled without
screws and without glue, using only the molded grooves
and wooden pegs. The chair has never been industrially
produced.*

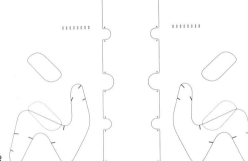

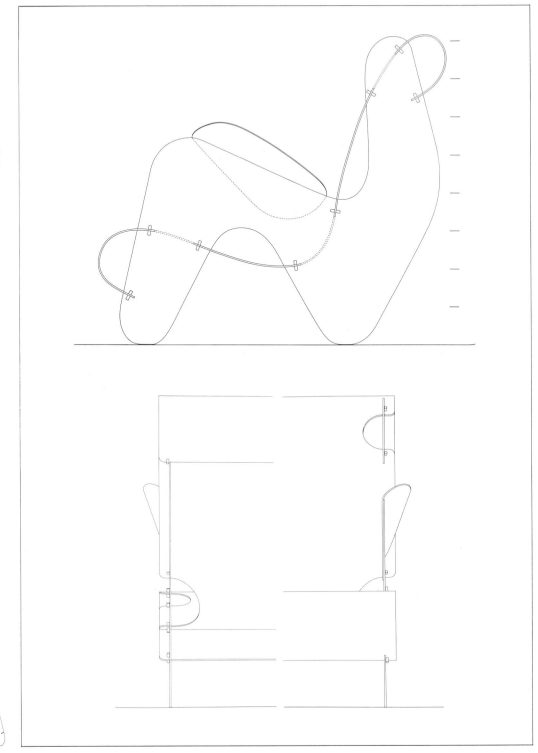

128

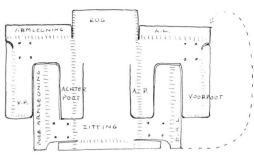

INGESNEDEN FIBER PLAAT, DIE WEEK GEMAAKT, GEBOGEN EN IN EEN VORM GEPERST EN GEDROOGD WORDT

EERSTE MODEL

Above: *the Birza-fauteuil, 1927;* at the top of the page: *the method of molding the armchair out of a single sheet of fiber or plywood.*

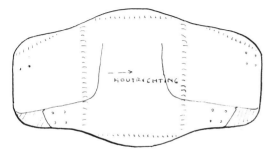

UITSLAG TRIPLEX STOEL

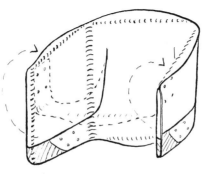

GEPERSTE GRONDVORM, DIE WORDT INGEZAAGD DE ZITTING OPGEBOGEN EN MET KLINKNAGELTJES BEVESTIGD

Stoel, 1927. Another model of an armchair molded out of a single curved sheet.

129

24. ALUMINUM-FAUTEUIL (Chair bent from one piece), 1942.
Molded aluminum sheeting; 60×48×72 cm.

Exh.: Milan, 1951; Amsterdam, 1971; London, 1972.

Repr.: A. Evers, 1946; *Open Oog*, 1946; *Domus*, 1951; *Wonen*, 1956; W. Sandberg, 1957; T. M. Brown, 1958; *Cat. G. Rietveld architect*, 1971.

Coll.: Amsterdam, Stedelijk Museum.

This armchair was constructed in war time and seems to have been inspired by the seats used by pilots of military planes; even the material was not chosen haphazardly, but reflected the possibilities, the limits, and the aesthetics of the time.

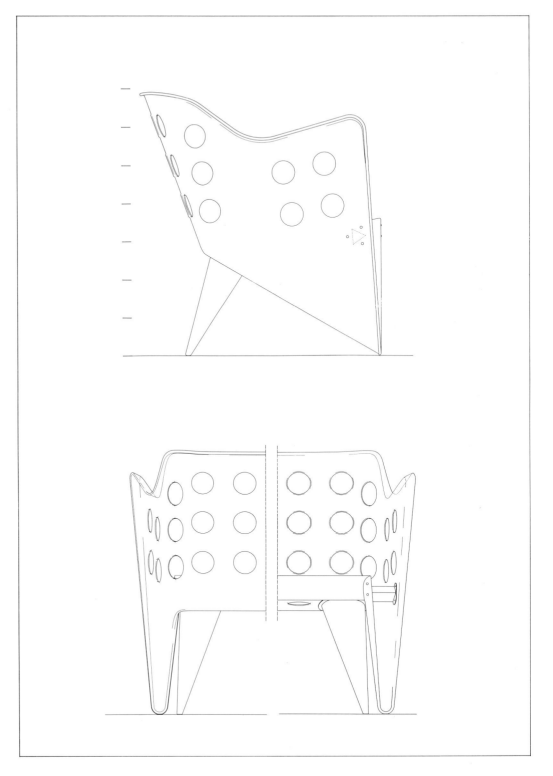

Verticals + Horizontals + Obliques = A New Chair

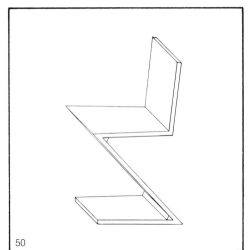

50

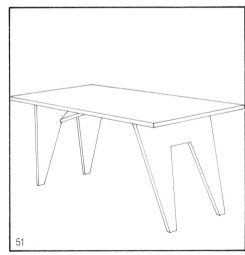

51

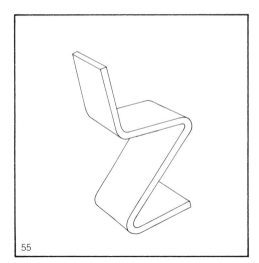

55

50. *Zigzag stoel, 1934.*
51. *Tafel, 1934.*
52. *Zigzag armstoel, 1942.*
53. *Zigzag armstoel, 1942, variant.*
54. *Zigzag kinderstoel.*
55. *Multiplex zigzag stoel, c. 1938, in curved plywood.*

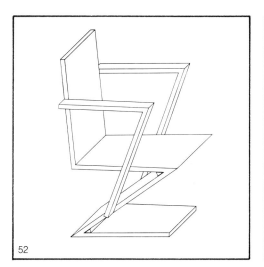

52

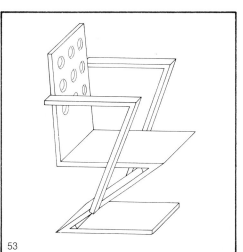

53

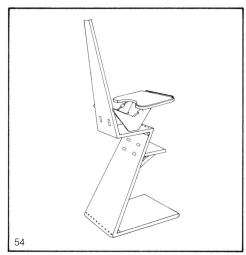

54

The slow metamorphosis of breaking up the object and later putting it together again according to new connotations had begun in Rietveld eleven years earlier with the "Berlijnse stoel" and the small painted table, both of 1923. Even at that stage the position of the chair legs was changed and they tended to become eliminated in an asymmetrical and unstable equilibrium; the small table was supported on two perpendicular planes crossing each other at 90°. It could therefore be imagined that with his continual experimentation Rietveld would sooner or later come to eliminate the legs altogether—even though none of his previous chairs could be properly described as having legs but rather supporting structures.

But there was more than this of interest in this new chair. He inserted a sloping plane which he interposed between the seat and base of the back for the precise purpose of introducing a powerful dynamic force into the composition.

It is not at all surprising that after the developments in his architectural work in the course of several years, and his association with the rationalist movement, his predilection for curved metal tubing in furniture should give way to a return to the use of wood in the "Zigzag" and *Krat* series. And in this return he continued the formal and structural analysis which he had begun so many years before.

The cycle of metal articles of furniture seemed to have come to an end. With the "Zigzag" chair Rietveld turned back again to two themes which he had neglected for some years: the return to the abstract and the return to wood. This change in style brought him back into relation with the De Stijl movement. Here we must take a step back in the history of

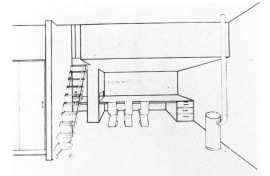

G. Rietveld, designs of interiors.

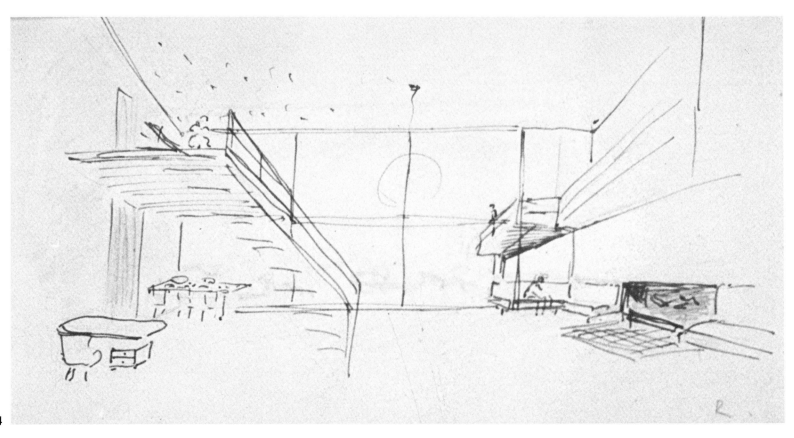

the movement to seek the source of the relationship which may have been unconscious but existed between this chair and certain principles of elementarism which had been formulated by Van Doesburg as far back as 1924. Writing in *De Stijl*, Van Doesburg explained his new theory as follows: "Elementary counter-composition adds to a rectangular and peripheral composition a new dimension, that of the oblique. From a realistic point of view, this resolves the tensions which are determined between the horizontal and vertical forces; sloping planes are introduced, dissonant planes which counterpose an architectonic and static structure to the force of gravity. In counter-composition the equilibrium of the plane plays a less important part. Each plane occupies a portion of the peripheral space, and the construction should be considered a phenomenon of tension rather than one of relationships among planes."[1]

At first Mondrian opposed the ideas of Van Doesburg, believing that he had so modified the previously stated principles of neoplasticism as to betray them, but later he too introduced the oblique line, not directly in his pictorial composition, but making the picture rotate at an angle of 45°. This new equilibrium built on the tension among vertical, horizontal, and oblique lines had automatically become a part of the De Stijl heritage.

It is in this context that we must see Rietveld's approach to the "Zigzag."

In addition to carrying out these principles, Rietveld's introduction of the oblique line brought into the vast panorama of chair design a completely new morphology which no one before him had ever imagined. The chair is formed out of four planes in a rhythmical sequence which develop in an elegant but apparently uneasy stability: back + seat + support + base, which in their turn describe one obtuse and two acute angles, concluding the surfaces in soft flowing lines.

From a more specifically technical viewpoint, it should be realized that Rietveld wished to make the chair in one piece, anticipating present-day mass production from a single mold, and seeking for ways which were still unknown at that time. Unlike the one-piece chairs designed in 1927 made out of a sheet of curved material, here the only thing which could have helped him was chemistry, after the discovery of giant molecules.

He chose wood, a medium with which he was already very familiar, and the variety he chose was elm. The back and seat were fitted by means of the comb system and two triangular wedges were set in the acute angles as a reinforcement between seat and base. In modern assembly techniques it would be possible to do without these wedges, without the risk of making the chair unstable or modifying its flexibility, but their presence now forms part of the actual image of the object.

According to the evidence of Van de Groenekan, Rietveld had a decided preference for a "rough" surface, "unsullied" by any kind of protective covering. He sometimes liked to bleach the wood with such natural agents as sunlight and sea salt deposit, as were used in the past in boat building. However, there are lacquered versions of this chair in white, red, and green: in the last case the perimeter line forming the border is white.

[1] Theo van Doesburg, in *De Stijl*, 75-76 (1926-27).

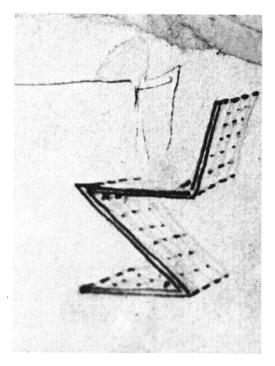

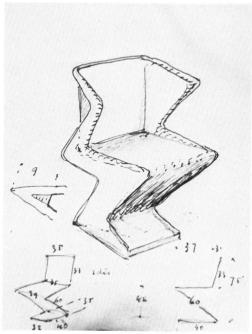

G. Rietveld, sketches showing variants of the Zigzag stoel.

25. ZIGZAGSTOEL (Zigzag chair), 1934.
Made of elmwood with an untreated surface;
37.5×43×73 cm.

Exh.: Milan, 1951; Utrecht, 1958; Rome, 1967;
Amsterdam, 1971; London, 1972.

Repr.: Bouwkundig Weekblad, 1935; *De 8 en
Opbouw*, 1935; *Domus*, 1951; T. M. Brown, 1958; H.
Honour, 1969; C. Meadmore, 1974.

Coll.: Amsterdam, Stedelijk Museum.

*The prototype was executed by G. van de Groenekan.
The chair was put into production by Metz & Co.
(Amsterdam, The Hague) after 1935.
There exist versions lacquered red or green, both edged
in white; they were used by Rietveld in the furnishing of
some country houses which he designed between 1938
and 1942.
Since 1971 the chair has been in regular production
under international license by Cassina, Meda.*

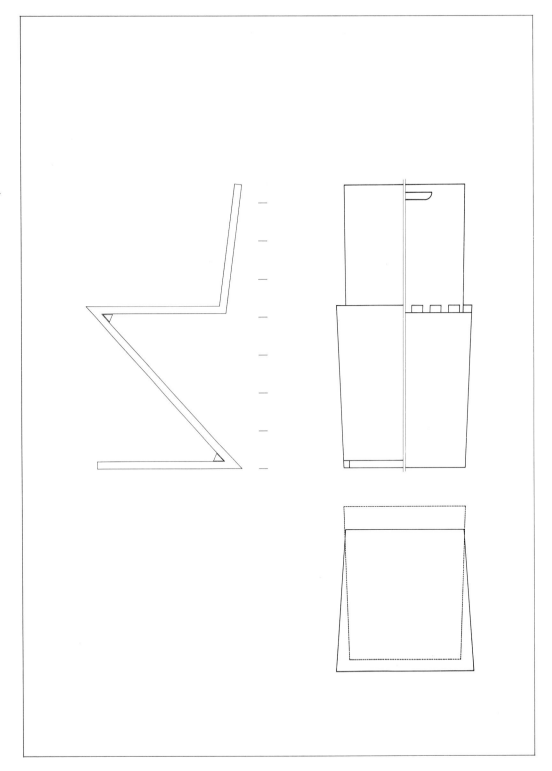

The group Zigzag stoelen en tafel, put into production
by Metz & Co. after 1935.

137

26. ZIGZAG ARMSTOEL (Armchair), 1934.
Made of elmwood with an untreated surface;
60×58×81 cm.

Repr.: *De 8 en Opbouw,* 1940; H. Honour, 1969.

Coll.: Utrecht, G. van de Groenekan.

The prototype was made by G. van de Groenekan.
Like the "Zigzag" chair, this armchair too was put
into production by Metz & Co. after 1935. It formed a
series with two variants of the same model, one with
the back perforated (6 large holes), the other with a
higher chair back.

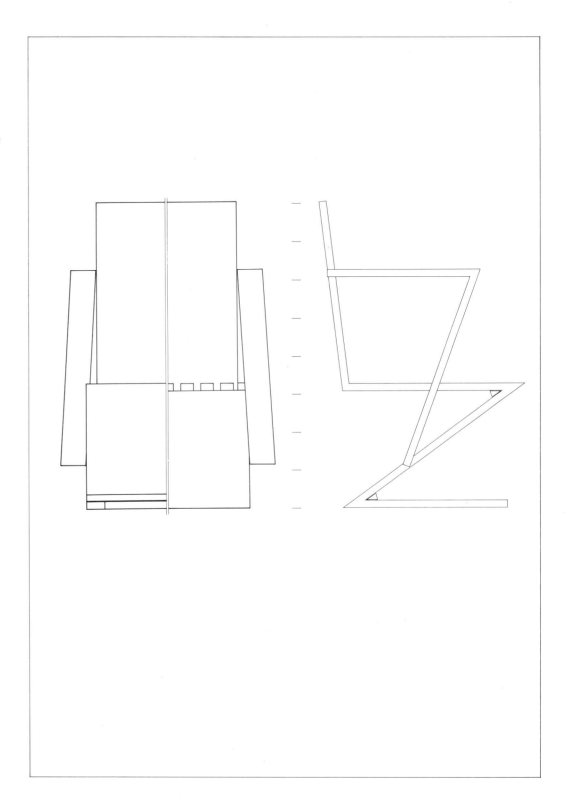

Exhibition in the shop window of Metz & Co.,
Amsterdam, 1940.

139

The "Poor Art" Object

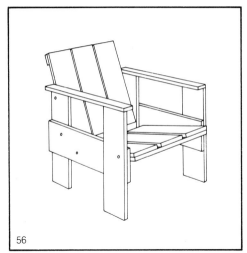

56

57

61

56. Kratstoel, 1934.
57. Krat tafel, 1934.
58. Krat boekenkast, 1934.
59. Krat tafel, 1934, variant.
60. Krat bureaustoel, 1934.
61. Tafel, 1934.
62. Krat schrijftafel, 1934.

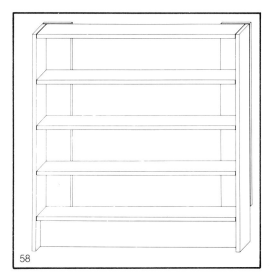

58

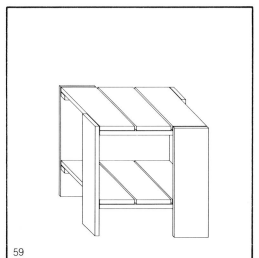

59

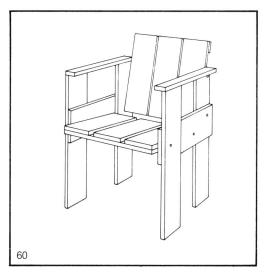

60

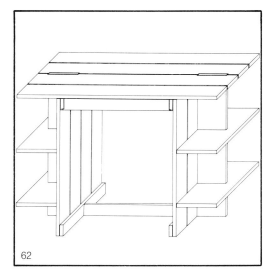

62

Whereas in the past Rietveld had bent all his efforts toward the purification of form and the search for pure abstraction, by liberating form from any kind of superstructure he now introduced a concrete material quality into the object as a fundamental value, granting the material the same importance as that of the other elements such as form, function, and color.

Here the dominant presence of wood acquired a connotative significance which was far different from that attributed to it in other previously created objects, and this led to a new perception of the object itself.

As well as taking his inspiration from an object which denotes other functions, such as a packing case, there was an intentional invitation to the ready-made; a tendency toward resemantization; the exploitation of an apparently insignificant object which could be transformed into another with precise connotations.[1]

The *Krat* system, originally intended for the furnishing of weekend houses, came to be seen as a highly valid alternative to traditional forms of furniture, and in the thought of its designer there was certainly the intention of developing a global project. With this design Rietveld entered the realm of "organic" design, which had in Alvar Aalto its greatest exponent, and was developed later by other Scandinavians too.

In architecture, also, his rationalist works, which had by now become firmly established, were alternated with works inspired by ethnography, especially in the case of country homes where he adopted local traditions in employing materials which were far from rationalist, such as straw for the roof and wood for the exterior.

This surprising and contrasting pluralism became a characteristic of Rietveld's design during this period. But the main factor to turn his attention to these choices was without any doubt the economic crisis which became acute in the second half of the 1930s and affected the building industry with high costs and shortage of materials.

The motive behind Rietveld's choice of design was plain. He wished to offer a vast public useful and inexpensive objects with basic structures. By the year 1934 the crisis had affected all world societies and governments. In this highly dramatic situation Rietveld found the means of expressing in significant terms his message as a working designer: he provided low-cost furniture made out of precut wooden parts of poor quality wood such as is usually employed for packing cases (from where the name *Krat*[2] derived) and so simple in form that the pieces could be quickly assembled by means of a few screws, without any joints or grooves. As in a game, each of the parts reflected a precise logic and each of the components acted as a dynamic support to the others, in a continuous rhythmical sequence.

But another aim of Rietveld was to urge the user to be creative himself by involving him in the planning process at the time when these toy-objects were assembled. Once again he showed that what mattered to him was the method of making an object which would illuminate and nurture the technological aspect and at the same time stimulate the imagination of the individual. Yet these objects, which seem to have been the origin of the American do-it-yourself fashion, were actually conceived as a potential stimulus to industrialization. Like all the De Stijl group, Rietveld always believed firmly in the liberating potential of the machine.

As Robert van't Hoff expressed it: "We must demand from the machine the maximum of work, from the worker the minimum, and the worker must in no way be involved in the personal caprices of the designer."[3]

But let us see what this habitat could be, the ideal environment in which to place this furniture. It could be imagined that the envelope which could surround the space would be primordial and archaic and would have the function of enhancing the object. Does the

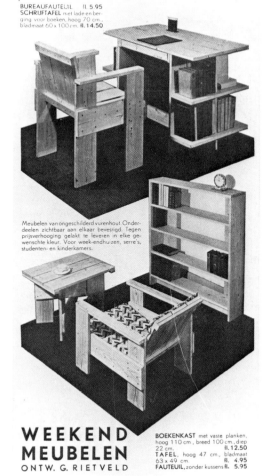

Advertisement page of the firm Metz & Co. for the Krat *furniture series, 1935.*

BUREAUFAUTEUIL fl. 5.95
SCHRIJFTAFEL met lade en berging voor boeken, hoog 70 cm., bladmaat 60 x 100 cm. fl. 14.50

Meubelen van ongeschilderd vurenhout. Onderdeelen zichtbaar aan elkaar bevestigd. Tegen prijsverhooging gelakt te leveren in elke gewenschte kleur. Voor week-endhuizen, serre's, studenten- en kinderkamers.

WEEKEND MEUBELEN
ONTW. G. RIETVELD

BOEKENKAST met vaste planken, hoog 110 cm., breed 100 cm., diep 22 cm. fl. 12.50
TAFEL, hoog 47 cm., bladmaat 63 x 49 cm. fl. 4.95
FAUTEUIL, zonder kussens fl. 5.95

effect after which Rietveld was aiming perhaps mirror the thought expressed in dogmatic terms by Van Doesburg many years earlier? ''No decoration, nothing superfluous, nothing artistic in the sense that it should empahsize a beauty added from the exterior, after the object had been produced. Only the sincerity of the object, in itself. Over and above everything, truth, function, construction, and no defect determined by an individualistic reflection.''[4] Thus it was the value of the object itself which counted, as an ethical and social rather than aesthetic value; the social value of art whose point of reference was life itself.

Having touched on this argument, one cannot overlook another which is of fundamental importance to the comprehension of Rietveld's thought. In an environment based on a form inspired from the constructive concept of the packing crate, there seems to be implied a controversial attitude, as we would see it today, when this environment is contrasted with the traditional middle-class model.

However, Rietveld did not use this design as the basis of speculation and mystification. As always he worked in a philosophical atmosphere which through the medium of De Stijl had become translated into an everyday reality, and he was unconcerned as to whether or not he was engaged in a revolutionary gesture. His ultimate purpose remained the construction by means of plastic art of a model of life which would be at the same time elementary and universal. When, moreover, we wish to consider the question of art in relation to class problems, we find again an answer in Van Doesburg: ''Art as we postulate it is neither proletarian nor bourgeois. It develops forces sufficiently efficacious to influence the whole of culture, instead of being influenced in its turn by class relationships.''[5]

The series initially consisted of: a small armchair (plate 27) whose prototype which most closely corresponds to the original design is to be found in the possession of his cabinetmaker and assistant Van de Groenekan; a small table (plate 28); and a bookcase

(plate 30), published for the first time in *De 8 en Opbouw* in April 1935. He later added to these: a dining chair (plate 31), of which a prototype is in the Centraal Museum, Utrecht; a desk (plate 33) and a variant of a small table (plate 29), both in the collection of the Stedelijk Museum, Amsterdam; a dining table, of which a copy is owned by Van de Groenekan and was placed by Rietveld in the Breukelerveen Zomerhuis.

It is possible that Rietveld planned to make some more pieces; we cannot help wondering, for example, why there was no design for a bed in this series. But so far research has not led to any positive conclusion.

This series of furniture was constructed out of a number of deal boards, measuring 18 mm. in thickness, 14.5 cm. in width, and obviously of variable lengths.

The continuous crisscrossing of lines and their projection beyond the object into space represents a characteristic principle employed by Rietveld from the time of his first pieces, beginning with the "Rood Blauwe," although the underlying conception of space may have varied. But the method of constructing the boards in planes and surfaces reminds us of the structural conception of the "Berlijnse stoel," that is, with a tendency to terminate in more closed volumes. The method of constructing by means of lines extending into space seems to have been abandoned forever.

Even the problem of packaging was dealt with by Rietveld in terms of rationalism and probably influenced his research into form. The various parts were subdivided into planes and contained in flat forms taking up very little space, just like real packing crates.

G. Rietveld, Zomerhuis at Loosdrechtsche Plassen, 1940, interior.
The house stands in a marshy landscape to the northwest of Utrecht. The architecture is rustic and inspired by the local tradition. Of particular interest is the floor made of painted blue oak circles; on the opposite page: drawing by Rietveld portraying the Verrijn-Stuart house at Breukelerveen, 1941.

---

[1] To a reader who asked him to explain this furniture, Rietveld wrote in *Bouwkundig Weekblad* in rather ironical terms, pointing out that people sometimes receive an object they consider precious, packed in a *Krat*, and do not know how to value the quality of the latter which probably contains in itself a significance, whether of material or communication, superior to the actual contents.
[2] *Crate* in English.
[3] Published in *De Stijl*, V, 12 (December 1922).
[4] Theo van Doesburg, in *De Stijl*, VI, 2 (April 1923).
[5] Theo van Doesburg, in *De Stijl*, V, 3 (March 1922).

27. KRATSTOEL (Crate furniture, chair), 1934.
Red spruce with untreated surface; 60×62×65 cm.

Exh.: Utrecht, 1958; Amsterdam, 1971; London, 1972.

Repr.: *De 8 en Opbouw*, 1935; G. Rietveld, 1935; T. M. Brown, 1958; P. Overy, 1969; *Casa Vogue*, 1974.

Coll.: Amsterdam, Stedelijk Museum; Utrecht, G. van de Groenekan.

Panels required:
10   14.5×45 cm.
2   14.5×60 cm.
2   5.5×45 cm.
2   5.5×49 cm.
2   5.5×60 cm.

This chair was meant to be upholstered in wool lined with printed canvas. Rietveld selected the fabric from the samples of Metz & Co. and his selection was by no means haphazard in view of the rigorously neoplastic pattern of repeated diagonal rectangles and the primary colors used. The designer of the fabric was Bart van der Leck who had been working on fabrics since 1919, which were not put into production until around 1928 by Metz & Co., the same firm which in 1934 produced this same armchair, as well as the chair, small table, bookcase, and desk belonging to the same series. These articles could be acquired lacquered in the colors chosen by the client. The armchair and all the other furniture in this series are now produced in deal under an international license by Cassina, Meda.

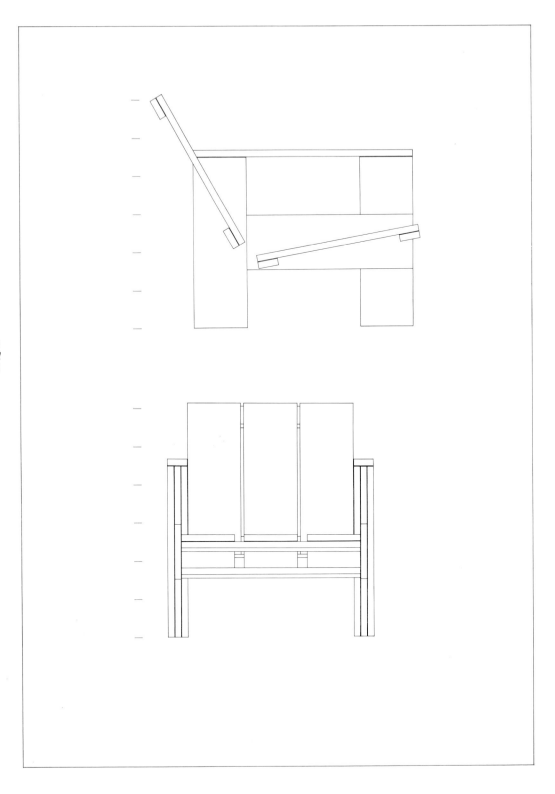

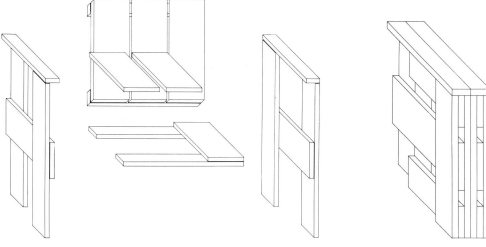

On the left: *the armchair ready for assembly, and packed ready for shipment.*

147

28:, 29. KRAT TAFEL (Crate furniture, small table), 1934.
Made of red spruce with untreated surface;
60×45×47 cm.; 47×47×45 (smaller variant).

Exh.: Amsterdam, 1971; London, 1972.

Repr.: *De 8 en Opbouw*, 1935; T. M. Brown, 1958; P. Overy, 1969; *Casa Vogue*, 1974.

Coll: Amsterdam, Stedelijk Museum.

Panels required:
First table:
5   14.5×60 cm.
4   14.5×45 cm.
2   5.5×45 cm.

Second table:

10   14.5×45 cm.
4   5.5×45 cm.

The second table, here shown as a variant, is believed unpublished.

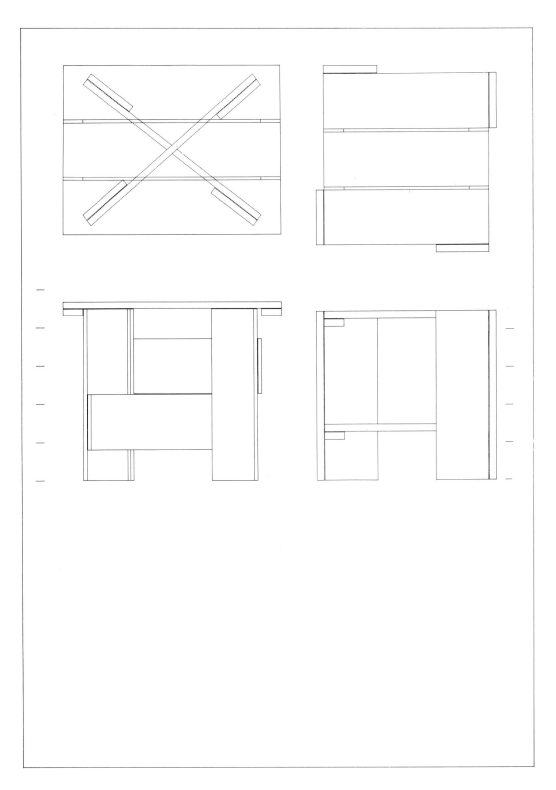

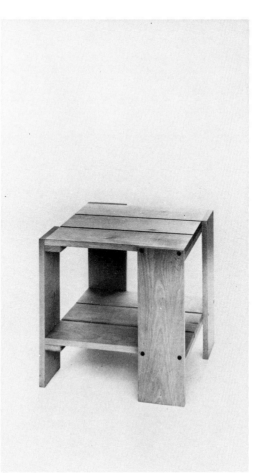

30. KRAT BOEKENKAST (Crate furniture,
bookcase), 1934.
Made of red spruce with untreated surface;
109×105×16.5 cm.

Repr.: De 8 en Opbouw, 1935; T. M. Brown, 1958;
Casa Vogue, 1974.

Panels required:
8   14.5×105 cm.
2   14.5×90 cm.

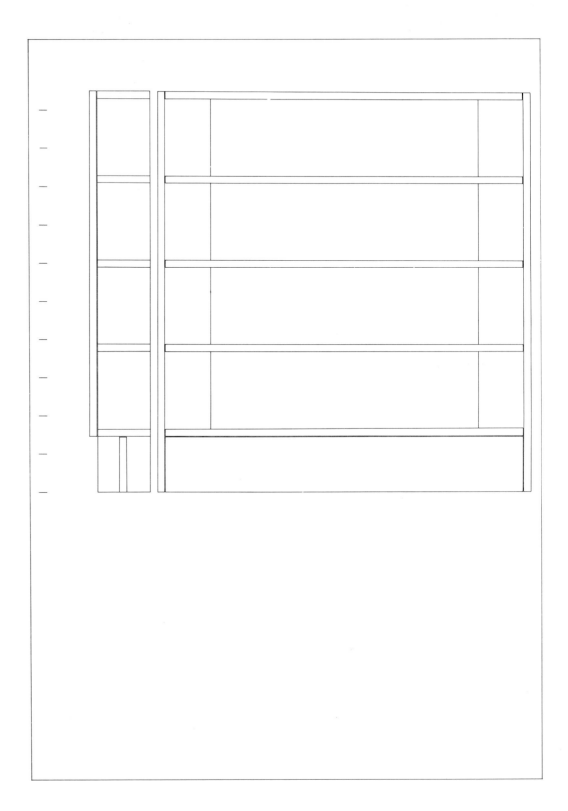

31.   KRAT BUREAUSTOEL (Crate furniture, chair), 1934.
Made of red spruce with untreated surface; 58×60×78 cm.

Exh: Utrecht, 1958.

Repr.:   *Casa Vogue*, 1974.

Coll.:   Utrecht, Centraal Museum.

Panels required:
6   14.5×40 cm.
4   14.5×62 cm.
2   14.5×50 cm.
4   5.5×50 cm.
2   5.5×46 cm.

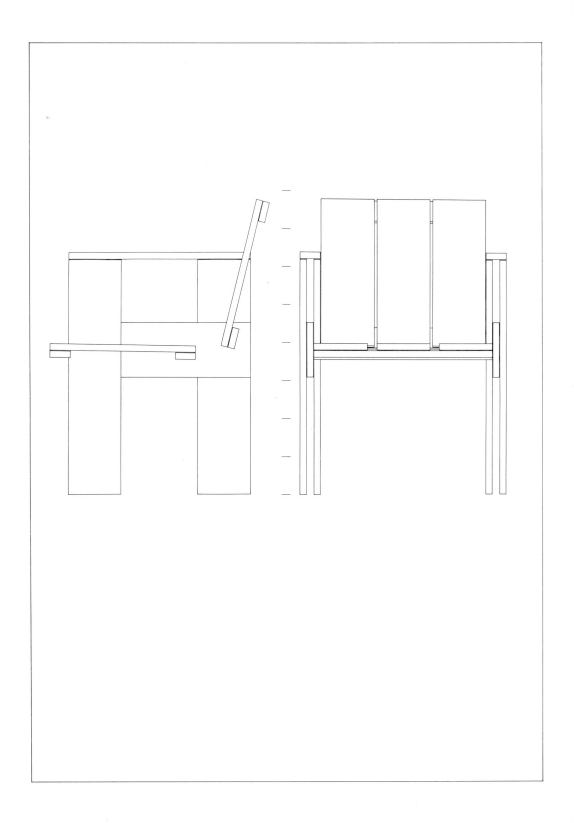

39.   TAFEL (Crate furniture, table), c. 1934.
Made of red spruce with untreated surface;
175×76×70 cm.

Repr.:   *De 8 en Opbouw*, 1941; T. M. Brown, 1958;
Casa Vogue, 1974.

Coll.:   Utrecht, G. van de Groenekan.

Panels required:
3   25×175 cm.
4   14.5×77 cm.
2   14.5×23 cm.
2   14.5×76 cm.

*This table did not form part of the series put into
production by Metz & Co. It was designed by Rietveld
for some country houses, including the house in
Breukelerveen of 1941.
Execution by G. van de Groenekan.*

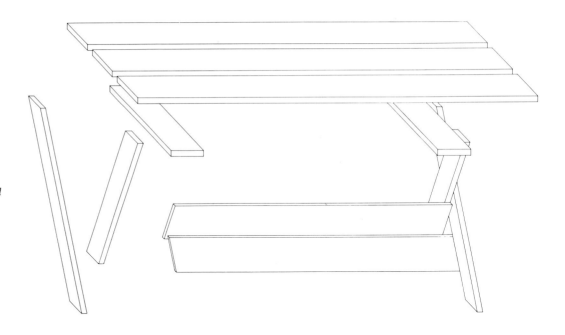

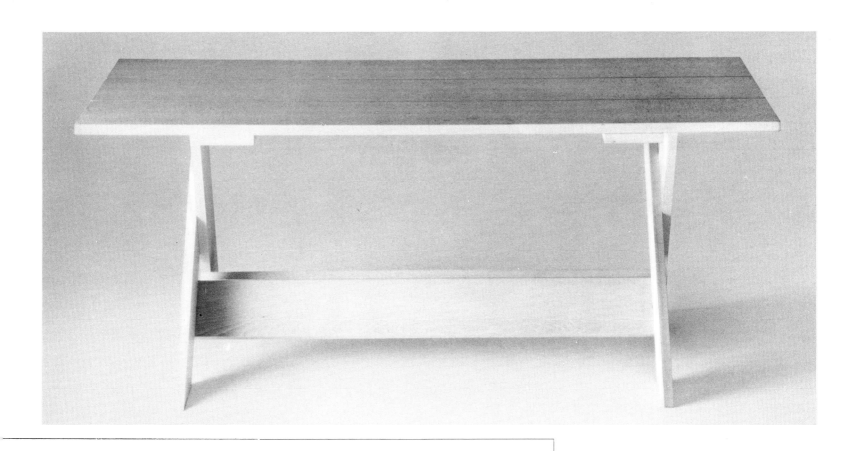

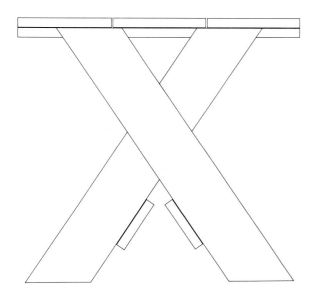

Interior of the Weekend Huis with the Krat tafel and Zigzag stoelen, published in De 8 en Opbouw, *no. 23, 1938.*

155

33.   KRAT SCHRIJFTAFEL (Crate furniture, desk),
1934.
Made of red spruce with untreated surface;
100×60×70 cm.

Repr.: Casa Vogue, 1974.

Coll.:   Amsterdam, Stedelijk Museum.

Panels required:
10   14.5×68 cm.
4   14.5×100 cm.
4   14.5×60 cm.
4   5.5×60 cm.
1   5.5×80 cm.
1   5.5×72×36 cm. (drawer).

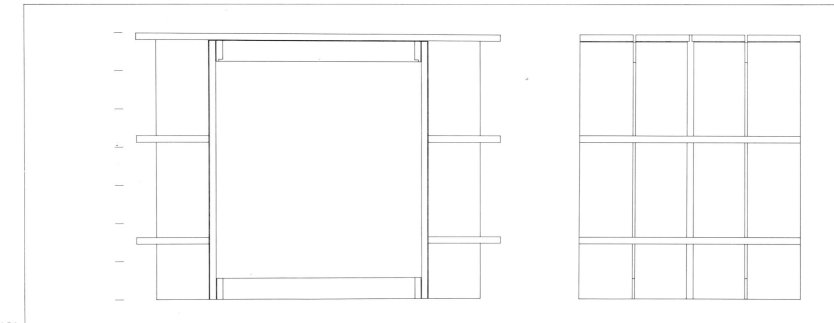

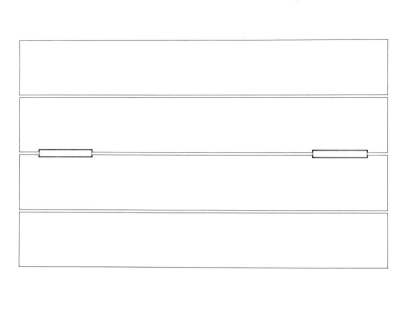

International Recognition

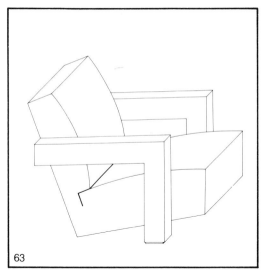

63

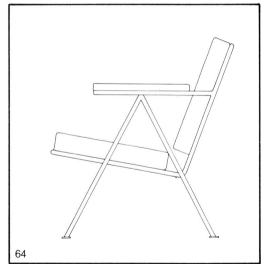

64

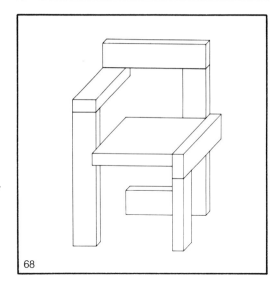

68

63. *Fauteuil, 1935.*
64. *Fauteuil, 1949, in polished metal with foam rubber upholstery.*
65. *Lage stoel, 1950, chair for primary schools in curved fiber.*
66. *Stoel, 1957, in metal and plastic (made with the collaboration of his son Wim).*
67. *UNESCO-fauteuil, 1958.*
68. *Steltman stoel, 1963.*

65

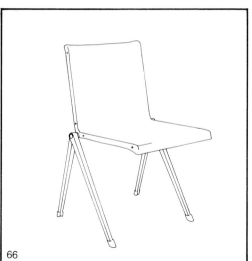

66

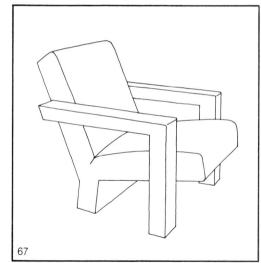

67

G. Rietveld (with his son Wim), design for Nagele, Noordoostpolder (not executed), 1954.
Below and bottom right: perspective view, ground plan, and sketches for the interior of the Nieuwe Volkswoning, 1941.

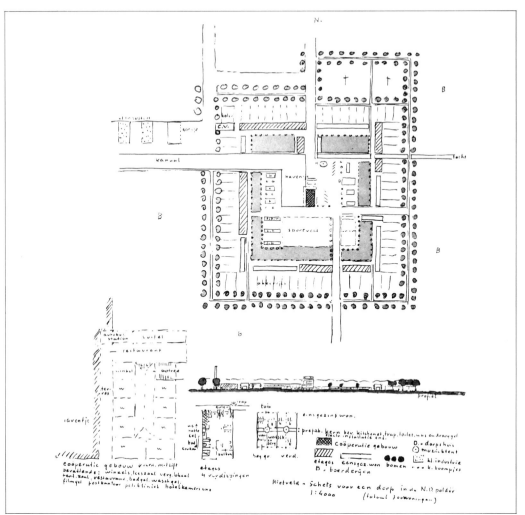

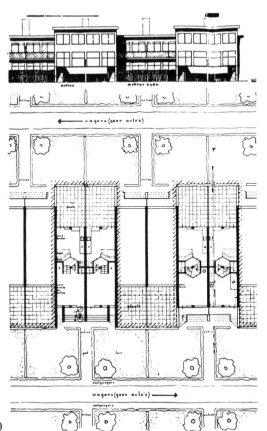

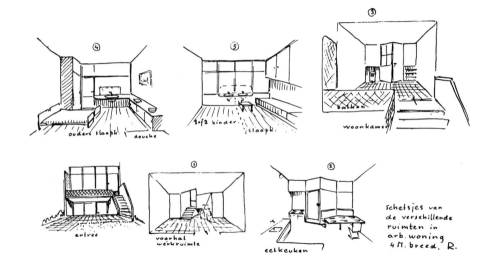

The Second World War had been over for some years and Rietveld was struggling to obtain commissions which would bring him to the attention of the critics once more. His country was urgently engaged in the reconstruction of the large cities which had been devastated by bombing. Government contracts naturally went first to all those who had previously distinguished themselves in the field of urban planning. Although Rietveld had been one of the founding members of the CIAM at La Sarraz and had taken part in important international exhibitions such as the Werkbund Siedlung in Vienna, he was still not very well known in the Netherlands and was therefore excluded from the work of reconstruction of the country.

It was only after 1950 that notice was taken of him by political administrators as an architect and artist, and from that time onward he was given more and more frequent public commissions, especially exhibition pavilions or representative works of architecture. As a result of this, a most busy period of architectural activity began when he was past the age of sixty. He tried to confirm and possibly amplify the spatial and structural achievements of his years of association with rationalism and neoplasticism.

In 1951 he was asked to organize a retrospective De Stijl exhibition in the Stedelijk Museum, Amsterdam. The same exhibition travelled to the Venice Biennale the following year and to the Museum of Modern Art in New York. He himself was represented in this exhibition with some pictures of the Schröder Huis and his famous furniture, designed between 1918 and 1925.

In this period he also arranged displays for the International Fairs at Utrecht. In 1951 he

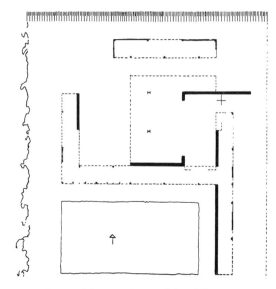

Two views and the ground plan of the exhibition pavilion for sculpture at Sonsbeek, Arnhem, designed by Rietveld in 1954.

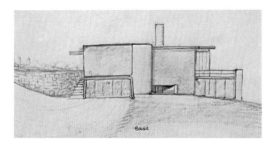

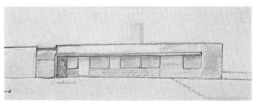

G. Rietveld, *designs for villas,* c. 1958; below: *villa at Oberlin, Ohio, 1958.*

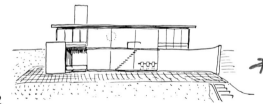

designed a home for spastic children in Curaçao, which he did not complete. The exhibition pavilion in Mexico City named *Aquí está Holanda* was produced in the following year.

Of his semipermanent architecture one of the most interesting buildings was a bicycle shed (Utrecht, 1953), now destroyed, where he used to support the roof a sequence of perpendicular beams joined so as to project from each other, in a system of building which was not dissimilar from the one he used in his famous "Rood Blauwe"; he then concluded the construction with some mass-produced sections to form the perimeter walls.

The Sonsbeek Pavilion

In 1954 Rietveld put up in Sonsbeek Park, Arnhem, an exhibition pavilion for a temporary international sculpture show; this must be viewed as one of his most representative works. The construction was in the form of a shelter extending into the natural landscape and bringing it inside itself. Wooden beams were used for the sheds, with a similar technique as was used for the Utrecht bicycle shed, and they were then inlaid with glass panels. The walls were formed of planes of fossilized wood used in the same way as perforated small bricks. These walls not only created a most unusual visual and textural effect, which immediately situated the work of architecture in the same scale of values as that of sculpture, but also created filters through which the light could pass with an effect of transparency. Building and sculpture complemented each other and were each reflected in the other's image. In order to grasp the full spatial significance of this work, we must remind ourselves of the ideas previously arrived at by Rietveld in the Schröder Huis, where he caused space to live, imposed on it a rhythm of its own, a personal structure which enables us to experience it as a human kind of space. As Rietveld said in one of his aphorisms as early as 1928: "The sole reality architecture can create is space."[1] He tended to circumscribe space, marking out a portion of it so as to create an awareness of space, and strived to explore the frontiers of spatialism in order to enlarge its field.

In Sonsbeek, however, he treated space without defining it, and in fact exaggerated the flowing movement running between the interior and exterior. Without being aware of it, the visitor passes from half-closed space into open space by way of a preordained route. To complete the structure Rietveld employed physical forces which had never before been brought into play in architecture. The perimeter of the pavilion ended in a curtain of hot air, which came into conflict with climatological factors.[2] The similarity in the ground plan, the abstract quality of planes and pilasters, the multiplicity of viewpoints, lead us inevitably to the Barcelona pavilion by Mies van der Rohe of 1929, but here its poverty, and at the same time its material concreteness, and the way it was integrated into nature, gave it a different accent, placing it in the sphere of the influence of Wright. Organic form, viewed as the spirit of simplification, of the decantation of forms and structures, and culminating in the conquest of four-dimensional space.

Also in 1954, Rietveld was made responsible for the Dutch pavilion at the Venice Biennale. In the same year he undertook the *Nagele* project (in collaboration with his son Wim, but never executed) for a new housing district on a polder, a new area of land reclaimed from the sea. He arranged for all services and amenities for the community to be provided, including a small harbor connected to the open sea through a canal. The square ground plan was rigorously neoplastic and the homes were made to gravitate around the central nucleus, projecting into the urban dimension the concept previously adopted in the *Kern Huizen* project. In 1954 he also built the Driessen Tile Company Showroom in Arnhem. In 1956 he took part in work on a new entry to the *Julianahal,* the Utrecht Fair, and built the textile factory De Ploeg in Bergeyk. The Hoograven houses in

Utrecht were built in 1954–57; in 1956–57 Rietveld built the Academie voor Beeldende Kunsten in Arnhem and the Instituut voor Kunstnijverheidsonderwijs en Industriële Vormgeving in Amsterdam. In 1957 he built the Dutch section of the Milan Triennial, reconstructed the interior of the Rijks Academie van Beeldende Kunsten in Amsterdam, and designed the press room for UNESCO in Paris; in collaboration with the engineer Boks of the firm of Bakema & Van der Broek, he built the Dutch pavilion in the Brussels Expo, the houses at Reeuwijk-Brug, and the offices for Schrage's Betonmij in Zwolle. He also designed the furnishings for the Friendship aircraft of the Fokkerfabrieken and for a KLM plane as well.

This represented his public activity up to 1958. We must not forget too that from 1949 to 1958 he built many private houses, the best known of which were the Velp houses of 1951, the Bergeyk of 1956, and the Apeldoorn of 1957, all built in the functional style, but with an even greater emphasis on neoplasticism than he introduced into his prewar houses. The various parts of the houses flowed into each other forming a perfect continuity.

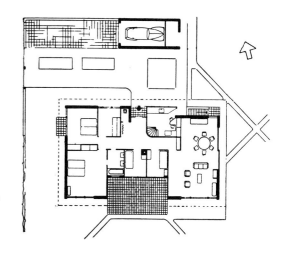

The Moment of Vindication
This chronicle of events has purposely been closed at 1958, the year of his seventieth birthday, because it was in this year that he received important recognition. A retrospective exhibition of his work was held in the Centraal Museum, Utrecht,[3] and at the same time the most important biography concerning him was published, by the American Theodore Brown, which became an essential work of reference for any further research. This was when Rietveld the "poet" was rediscovered, and all the architectural periodicals of the world wrote about him and presented his works to the public.

This automatically initiated a new period, when commissions followed more consistently. He undertook some work for Americans, such as the Parkhurst House in Oberlin, Ohio, and the Ilpendam House of 1958–59, which was without doubt one of the best conceived of all his houses, organized throughout on horizontal lines.

Under the pressure of this increasing number of commissions, he decided to enlarge his studio and in January 1961 was joined by Van Dillen[4] and Van Tricht who from then on worked with Rietveld on all his projects. Together with them he executed works previously designed—the Institute of Applied Arts in Amsterdam[5] and the Arnhem Academy; he constructed the hall of the Hoofddorp Cemetery (1958–66, design by Rietveld, execution by Van Dillen), the conference building in Amsterdam, 1964–67

Villas built by Rietveld. Above and below: the Huis Stoop at Velp, 1951; bottom left: the Huis van den Doel at Ilpendam, 1958-59.

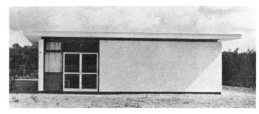

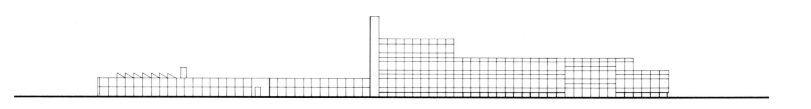

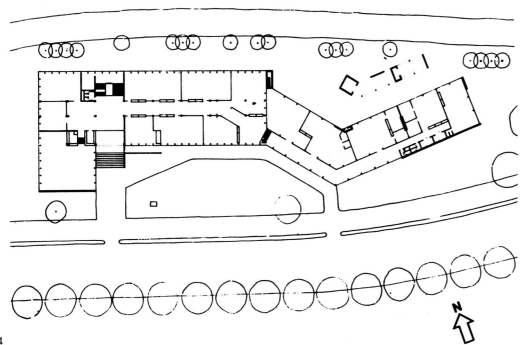

G. Rietveld, perspective views, ground plan, and photograph of the Akademie voor Beeldende Kunst en Kunstnijverheid Onderlangs, Arnhem.

164

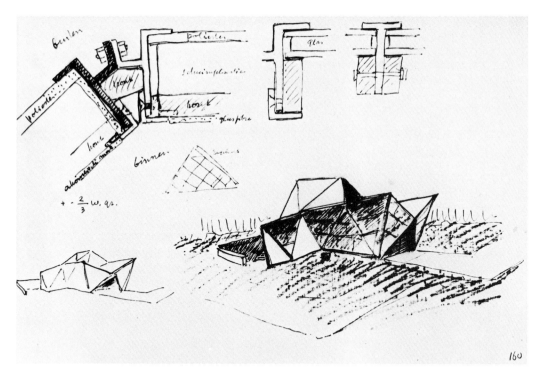

(design by Rietveld, execution by Van Tricht), the Protestant Church Zijdelveld Uithoorn, 1960–65 (design by Rietveld and Van Tricht, execution by Van Dillen and Van Tricht), and the Rijksmuseum Vincent van Gogh in Amsterdam, 1963–74, the last great project in which Rietveld took a direct part. Although in this case it was on a gigantic scale, we find here again the marks of other of his works of architecture, not least among them the Dutch pavilion at the Venice Biennale. Closed cube forms, varied only by some panes of glass, were interconnected and integrated around the central body which was glazed all over and contained the staircases. Inside, a series of terraces project form the perimeter walls, surrounding a large, empty central space. A particularly interesting feature was the large skylight constructed out of transparent pyramid-shaped forms, supported by a metal pyramid structure at an angle of 45° to the panes. This work was completed by Van Tricht almost ten years after Rietveld's death and its color scheme did not fulfill the original intentions of the architect as it was reduced almost to monochrome.

Parallel with all these public works were some important buildings Rietveld designed or executed privately. Among them were the Toonzaal Centrum Industriële Vormgeving,[6] Amsterdam, 1961–62; the Gemeente Huis Leerdam, 1962–63 (not executed); the elementary school in Badhoevedorp, 1958–65; the Heerlen house, 1961–64, where he obtained the maximum effect of transparency as compared with other houses previously constructed by him. The Stiltecentrum Technische Hogeschool in Twente or Center of Silence (1963, not executed), a large center where students could meet and work quietly, was to be a glass polyhedric structure with twenty sides, twenty meters in height, and a complete exception to the types of building in Rietveld's repertory, with their empahsis on simpler parts which were assembled.

In the last years of his life Rietveld sometimes turned again to furniture design, but more than anything this was to note down in sketch form some variants of articles created in the

165

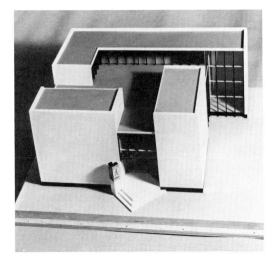

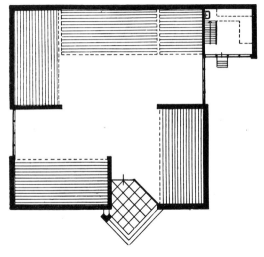

G. Rietveld, model and ground plan of the Dutch pavilion at the Venice Biennale, 1954.

past, differing either in form or in some details of construction.

A few months before his death,[7] he remodelled the Steltman jewellery shop in The Hague and placed there a new chair which he called the "Steltman stoel." This chair represented a further important development in his study of this article of furniture; its value is equal to that of the "Berlijnse stoel" and the "Zigzag." The chair is constructed out of wooden parallelepipeds forming together an L shape, according to the Cartesian axes, which project one out of the other in a rhythmical progression, until they form a ribbon running along the plane of the seat. As was the case with his last works of architecture, the idea was a perfect exemplification of neoplasticism and shows how Rietveld was the most representative architect of the De Stijl group in an absolute sense.

And like this architecture, the chair, too, has no focal center; from whichever side one looks at it, it takes on a new and surprisingly different identity. The various elements which compose it seem to define the space, but in reality they design it, allowing it then to flow freely among them.

But perhaps the secret and well justified ambition of Rietveld's last years was to have the opportunity to engage in town planning. Together with his students he did try to analyze the complexity of this field in relation to technology and the social sciences, making use of town planning and urban development projects and often deploring the limitations of building technology in the era of electronics and space flights.

In 1963 he was made an honorary member of the Association of Dutch Architects and was given an honorary degree at Delft Polytechnic University.

This was the epilogue of the life of a master, a master of urban design as well as of his other spheres of activity, a craftsman who made himself into a town planner and who in each of his projects always sought an atmosphere of equilibrium and neutrality, the better to serve man and his "environmental space."

In conclusion, Rietveld's own thoughts can give us the measure of his universal and pantheistic view of life, which always supported him, and his highly humanitarian approach. "Our creations represent only a small contribution toward the construction of our image of the world. This image of the world must certainly be linked to a particular human system. But our limited and channelled perceptions move within an immense unknown universe. So do I imagine that even those flat gray insects which live under stones have their own image of the world, an infinite image in terms of the animal system which pertains to them. I imagine that even flies, which live but one day, have their own idea of the infinite because it seems to me that every system is shut in and that outside it there is only nothingness without end. Even in the human system, each one of us is satisfied with his own image of a world in eternal expansion. But I believe that there are more people who accidentally test their own image than there are people to whom the joy is reserved of being knowingly present at the expansion of their own image of the world. To express such a joy is, in my opinion, the meaning of art. . . .It seems to me too that all our actions could be complementary to an eternal scheme which goes beyond our own system. . . .Viewed as a whole life is like a balance which is always looking for its center of gravity."[8]

[1] Gerrit Rietveld, *Inzicht*.
[2] This pavilion was reconstructed in 1964 by the Association of Dutch Architects in the park of the Rijksmuseum Kröller-Müller in Otterloo, on the occasion of the exhibition of Barbara Hepworth's sculpture.
[3] In nine rooms of the museum 89 works were exhibited including furniture and photographs of designs and buildings.
[4] Van Dillen died in 1966.
[5] Later named the "Gerrit Rietveld Academie."
[6] Destroyed in 1971.
[7] In Utrecht in June 1964.
[8] From an interview recorded in 1957 by Theodore M. Brown.

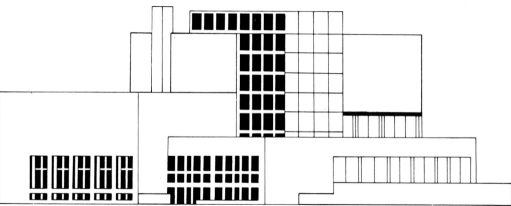

Rietveld's last work, completed by Van Tricht more than ten years after Rietveld's death: the Van Gogh Museum, Amsterdam, 1963-74.

Top left: a detail of the exterior with the central block containing the stairs; below: general view; top right: the special roof which produces an even light over the interior (above).

167

34. FAUTEUIL (Armchair), 1935.
Armchair with wooden structure and wool upholstery;
covered with brown *ecru* material, with visible
diagonal stitching; 68×86×67 cm.

Exh.: Amsterdam, 1971; London, 1972.

Repr.: T. M. Brown, 1958.

Coll.: Amsterdam, Stedelijk Museum.

*Designed for the production of Metz & Co.; this chair
was often used by Rietveld in the halls of public
buildings; in 1954 it was placed in the Showroom of the
Driessen Tile Company, Arnhem.*

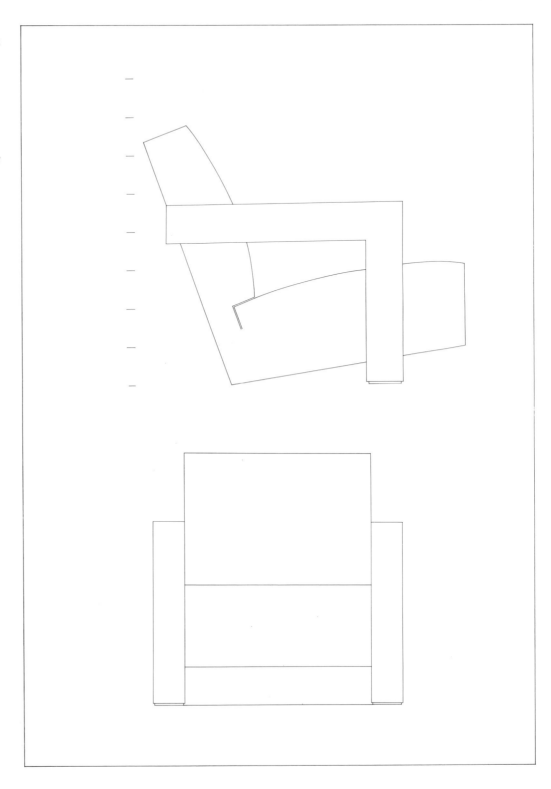

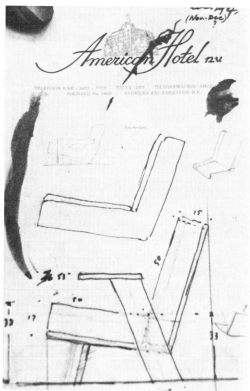

Sketch by Rietveld for a new armchair.

35. UNESCO-FAUTEUIL (Armchair), 1958.
Armchair with wooden structure entirely upholstered
in foam rubber and wool; covered in *écru* material;
74.5 × 80 × 80 cm.

Coll.:   Paris, UNESCO.

*Designed especially for the new press room of
UNESCO in Paris. In Rietveld's sketches the front
supporting structures, or sides, slope inward, creating
a trapezoidal figure in the front of the chair. However,
in the final version, the two sides were brought into
parallel position.*

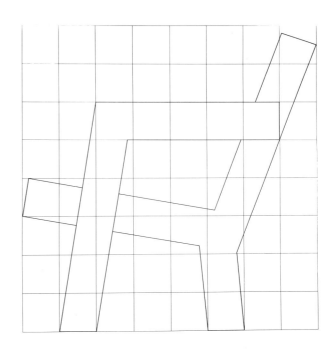

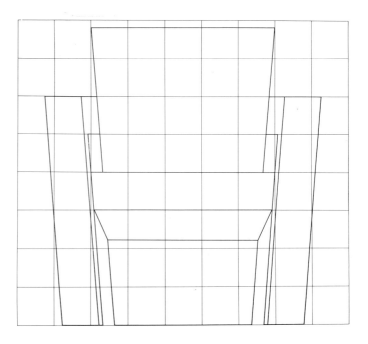

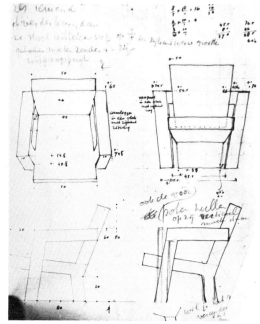

Sketch by Rietveld with annotations by UNESCO-fauteuil.

View of the press room of UNESCO, Paris.   171

36.   STELTMAN STOEL (Steltman chair), 1963.
Made of oak with untreated surface;
50×50×45×45×70 cm.

Exh.:   Amsterdam, 1971; London, 1972.

Repr.:   Cat. *G. Rietveld architect*, 1971; C.
Meadmore, 1974.

Coll.:   Amsterdam, Stedelijk Museum.

Created for the interior of the Steltman jeweller's shop,
The Hague; there also exists an upholstered version, as
was the case with the ''Berlijnse stoel.'' After
Rietveld's death, some versions in elm were made
which were upholstered, with whitened open-pore
surface, and others lacquered white.
The prototypes for the jeweller's shop were executed by
G. van de Groenekan.

Rietveld's notes for the construction of the Steltman stoel.

173

Exhibitions Referred to in the Notes to the Plates

1919
Haarlem, Museum van Kunstnijverheid.

1923
Berlin.
Weimar, Bauhaus.

1936
New York, Museum of Modern Art.

1951
Amsterdam, Stedelijk Museum [De Stijl exhibition].
Milan, Ninth Triennial.

1952
New York, Museum of Modern Art [De Stijl
exhibition].
Venice, Biennale.

1958
Utrecht, *Rietveld-tentoonstelling*, Centraal Museum.

1959
Amsterdam, Stedelijk Museum.

1967
Rome, Instituto Statale d'Arte.

1968
London, Camden Borough Council [De Stijl
exhibition].

1971
London, The Arts Council of Great Britain, Hayward
Gallery.

1973
Zürich, Kunstgewerbemuseum.

1975
Amsterdam, *Metalen Buisstoelen 1925-1940*, Stedelijk
Museum.

Bibliography

Works Referred to in the Notes to the Plates

1919
Doesburg, Theo van, in *De Stijl*, no. 11.
*Cat. Tentoonstelling, Aesthetisch uitgevoerde
gebruiksvoorwerpen*, Haarlem.

1920
Doesburg, Theo van, *Schilderkunst van Giorgio de
Chirico en een stoel van Rietveld*, in *De Stijl*, no. 5.
*Nederlandsche Ambachts-en Nijverheidskunst
Jaarboek*, Rotterdam.
*Proeve van kleurencompositie in interieur (1919),
Meubelen van G. Rietveld*, in *De Stijl*, no. 12.

1921
Oud, J. J. P., in *Bouwkundig Weekblad*, no. 11.

1922
De Stijl, no. 12.

1923
De Stijl, no. 5.
*Dokterskamer (uitgevoerd bij Dr. Den Hartogh te
Maarssen) door G. Rietveld*, in *De Stijl*, nos. 3, 4.
L'Architecture vivante, vol. 3.
Mert, no. 4.

1924
Boeken, A., *Bij-een paar afbeeldingen van werk G.
Rietveld*, in *Bouwkundig Weekblad*, no. 39.
Havelaar, J., "Het Moderne meubel," in *De
toegepaste kunsten in Nederland*, Rotterdam.
Taut, B., *Die Neue Wohnung*, Leipzig.

1925
Jansen, A. H., *Het industrieel uitgevoerde meubel*,

Rotterdam.
L'Architecture vivante, vol. 5.
Lissitzky and Arp, *Die kunstismen*.

1926
Lissitzky, El, "Architecture, Housing cultura," in
Stroitel naia Promyshlennost, no. 12, Moscow.
Oud, J. P. P., *Hollandische Architektur*, Munich.
De Stijl, nos. 75, 76.

1927
Holland, *Sier en Nijverheidskunst, 1900-1926*.
Rietveld, G., in *De Stijl*, nos. 79-84
Vouloir, no. 25.

1928
Binnenhuis, no. 5.
Schneck, A. G., *Der Stuhl*, Stuttgart.

1929
Grouwe, W. F., *Nederlandsche Ambachts-en
Nijverheidskunst Jaarboek*, Rotterdam.
Jong, J. de, *De nieuwe richting in de Kunstnijverheid in
Nederland*, Rotterdam.

1931
*Werk-Jaarboek van Nederlandsche Ambachts &
Nijverheidskunst 1930*, Rotterdam.

1932
Merkelbach, B., "Tentoonstelling bij de firma Metz &
Co. te Amsterdam," in *De 8 en Opbouw*, vol. 3.

1933
Platz, G. A., *Wohnräume der Gegenwart*, Berlin.

1934
Falkenberg-Liefrink, I., in *De 8 en Opbouw*.

175

1935
De 8 en Opbouw, no. 1.
"Interieur met meubelen van G. Rietveld," in
Bouwkundig Weekblad, November.
Weekend meubelen: ontw. G. Rietveld, in *De 8 en
Opbouw*, no. 8.

1936
Barr, A. H., *Cubism and Abstract Art*, Museum of
Modern Art, New York.

1940
Bodon, A., "Meubeltentoonstelling bij Metz & Co.,"
in *De 8 en Opbouw*, no. 11.

1941
De 8 en Opbouw, no. 8.

1946
Evers, A., in *Bouwkundig Weekblad*, no. 64.
Open Oog, no. 1.

1948
Giedion, S., *Mechanization Takes Command*, New
York.

1951
De Stijl, catalogue 81, Stedelijk Museum.
Domus, September.

1953
Zevi, B., *Poetica dell'architettura neoplastica*, Milan.

1954
Barr, A. H., *Master of Modern Art*, New York.
Pluym, W. van der, *Vijf eeuwen binnenhuis en meubels
in Nederland 1450-1950*, Amsterdam.

1956
Jaffé, H. L. C., *De Stijl: 1917-1931*, The Hague. *Wonen*.

1957
Sandberg, W., "Rietveld und seine Stühle," in *Form*,
no. 1.

1958
Brown, Theodore M., *The Work of G. Rietveld,
Architect*, Cambridge, Mass.

1959
Schaafsma, H., *Gerrit Rietveld: Bouwmeester van een
nieuwe tijd*, Utrecht.

1960
Banham, R., *Theory and Design in the First Machine
Age*, London.
"*Les sources du XXe siècle*," in *Les arts en Europe de
1884 à 1914*, Musée National d'Art Moderne, Paris.

1965
Architectural Design, no. 12.

Onck, A. van, "Metadesign," in *Edilizia Moderna*,
no. 85.

1967
Jaffé, H. L. C., *De Stijl*, Cologne.
Veronesi, G., "Il neoplasticismo e lo Stijl," in *L'arte
moderna*, no. 49, Milan.

1968
Fanelli, G., *Architettura moderna in Olanda,
1900-1940*, Florence.

1969
Honour, H., *Cabinet Makers and Furniture Designers*,
London.
Overy, P., *De Stijl*, London.

1971
Cat. G. Rietveld architect, Stedelijk Museum,
Amsterdam.

1973
Cat. Die Zwanziger Jahre-Kontraste eines Jahrzehntes,
Zürich.

1974
Casa Vogue, October.
Jong, H. de, *Stoelen*, Delft.
Meadmore, C., *The Modern Chair—Classics in
Production*, London.
Zevi, B., *Poetica dell'architettura neoplastica* (rev.
ed.) Turin.

1975
Cat. Metalen Buisstoelen 1925-1940, Amsterdam.
Cat. Rietveld Schröder Huis 1925-1975, Utrecht.

**Other Texts of Particular Interest in
Connection with Dutch Architecture and the
De Stijl Movement**

1925
Doesburg, Theo van, *Grundbegriffe der neuen
gestaltenden Kunst*, Munich.
Mondrian, P., *Neue Gestaltung*, Munich.

1930
Die Wohnung für das Existenzminimum, Frankfurt.

1932
Loghem, J. B. van, *Bouwen-Bauen-Batir-
Building/Holland/Nieuwe zakelijkheid-Neues
bauen—Vers une architecture réelle—Built to live in*,
Amsterdam.
Sartoris, A., *Gli elementi dell'architettura funzionale*,
Milan.
*Werkbundsiedlung internationale Ausstellung,
Katalog*, Vienna.

1932-5
"Moderne bouwkunst in Nederland," vols. V, VI, IX,
XII.

1935
Oud, J. J. P., *Nieuwe bouwkunst in Holland en
Europa*, The Hague.
Pica, A., "Nascita e fortune dell'architettura olandese
moderna," in *Emporium*, no. 491.

1937
*Hedendaagsche architectuur in Nederland—
Architecture hollandaise d'aujourd'hui—Holländische
Baukunst von heute—Dutch Architecture of Today*,
Amsterdam.

1938
Bierens, Haan D. de, *Schoonheid van het moderne
binnenhuis in Nederland*, Amsterdam.
Hausbrand, F., *Kleine landhuizen in Holland*,
Amsterdam.
"L'architettura mondiale," in *Casabella Costruzioni*,
no. 123.

1940
*Repertorium betreffende Nederlandsche monumenten
van geschiedenis en Kunst*, 2 vols., The Hague.

1941
Giedion, S., *Space, Time, and Architecture*,
Cambridge, Mass.

1950
Zevi, B., *Storia dell'architettura moderna*, Turin.

1953
Bakema, J. B., "Dutch Architecture Today," in
Architect's Year Book, no. 5, London.

1957
Blijstra, R., *Nederlandse bouwkunst na 1900*,
Amsterdam.

1959
Vriend, J. J., *Architectuur van deze eeuw*, Amsterdam.

1960
Benevolo, L., *Storia dell'architettura moderna*, Bari.

1961
Scully, V., *Modern Architecture*, New York.

1965
Jaffé, H. L. C., *The "De Stijl" Group*, Amsterdam.

1968
De Stijl, A Camden Festival Exhibition, London.
De Stijl, reprinted, in 3 vols., Amsterdam.

1973
Zevi, B., *Spazi dell'architettura moderna*, Turin.

Writings on Rietveld's Works

1919
Doesburg, Theo van, "Aanteekeningen bij een leunstoel van Rietveld," in *De Stijl*, no. 11.

1922
Boeken, A., "Eenige opmerkingen over de winkelverbouwing Kalverstraat 107 te Amsterdam: arch. G. Rietveld," in *Bouwkundig Weekblad*, no. 49.

1923
Boeken, A., "De Winkelpui Kalverstraat 107 te Amsterdam: architect G. Rietveld," in *Bouwkundig Weekblad*, no. 45.

1928
"Garage met chauffeurswoning: architect Rietveld," in *i 10*, no. 13.
"Interieur: Rietveld-Schräder," in *De Stijl*, nos. 85, 86.
"Moderne meubelinrichting: G. Th. Rietveld," in *Binnenhuis*, no. 17.
Tussenbroek, O. van, "Drie stoelen van G. Rietveld," in *Binnenhuis*, no. 5.

1931
Ravestejn, S. van, "Rietveld Huizen te Utrecht," in *Gemeenschap*, no. 10.

1933
Broek, J. H. van den, "Vragen aan Rietveld," in *De 8 en Opbouw*, no. 4.
Bromberg, P., "G. Rietveld bij Metz & Co.," in *Binnenhuis*, no. 20.
"Het bouwen te Haren: landhuis architect G. Rietveld," in *Bouwkundig Weekblad*.

1934
Hausbrand, F. "De nieuwe magazijnen voor huisinrichting van Metz & Co.," in "Den Haag: archs. Penaat, van der Leck en Rietveld," in *Bouwkundig Weekblad*.
Staal, A., "Vragen over de 'vragen' van Rietveld," in *De 8 en Opbouw*, no. 1.

1937
Buys, H., "Interieur met meubelen van G. Rietveld," in *Landhuis*.
Schnelling, H. G. J., "Nieuw werk van architect Rietveld," in *Bouwkundig Weekblad*, no. 5.

1940
"Architect Rietveld en een rieten dak," in *Utrechtsch Dagblad*, August.
Merkelbach, B., "Bij het werk van Rietveld," in *De 8 en Opbouw*, no. 11.

1941
Tussenbroek, O. van, in *Interieur*, no. 58.

1951
"Wohnhaus für einen Arzt in Kinderdijk: arch. Rietveld," in *Werk*, no. 11.

1953
"Rietveld, G. Th.," *Winkler Prins Encyclopaedie*, vol. 16, Amsterdam.

1954
"Nederland op de 27e Biennale: nieuwe paviljoen van architect Rietveld," in *Het Vaderland*, no. 33.

1955
"Complex van Rietveld is 'blikvanger van rondweg'," in *Nieuw Utrechts Dagblad*, August.
Mees, J., "Sonsbeek," in *Bouwkundig Weekblad*, nos. 31, 32.
"Sculpture Pavilion, Arnhem, Holland: G. Rietveld," in *Architectural Design*," no. 25.

1956
Baukunst und Werkform, no. 9.
Braat, L. P. J., "Rietveld's beeldhouwpavilijoen te Sonsbeek," in *Forum*, no. 11.
"Nieuw werk van G. Rietveld," in *De Groene Amsterdammer*, March.
"Sculpture Pavilion," in *Art & Architecture*, no. 3.

1958
Architect and Building News, June.
Brown, Theodore M., *The Work of G. Rietveld, Architect*, Cambridge, Mass.
Cat. Rietveld-tentoonstelling, Bijdrage tot de vernieuwing der bouwkunst, Utrecht, Centraal Museum.
"G. Th. Rietveld geb. 1888," in *Goed Wonen*, no. 6.
"G. Rietveld 70 jaar," in *Bouwkundig Weekblad*, no. 25.
"G. Rietveld 70 jaar," in *Forum*, no. 3. (This number is entirely devoted to Rietveld).
L'architettura: cronache e storia, no. 38.

1959
Schaafsma, H., *Gerrit Rietveld. Bouwmeester van een nieuwe tijd*, , Utrecht.
Roth, A., "L'oeuvre de Gerrit Rietveld," in *Architecture-Formes-Fonctions*, no. 6.

1961
"Rietveld," in *Selearte*, no. 50.

1963
Bekaert, G., "G. Th. Rietveld leeft voort," in *Streven*.

1964
Kunst in Utrecht.
Vriend, J. J., "G. Th. Rietveld 1888-1964," in *De Groene Amsterdammer*, July.
Werk, November.
Wilson, C. S., "Gerrit Rietveld: 1888-1964," in *Architectural Review*, vol. 136.

1965
Brown, Theodore M., "Rietveld's Egocentric Vision," in *The Society of Architectural Historians Journal*.
"G. Th. Rietveld 1888-1964," in *Bauen und Wohnen*, no. 11.

1966
Arquitectura (Argentina), no. 47.

1971
Cat. G. Rietveld architect, Stedelijk Museum, Amsterdam.
Ozinga, M. D., *Rietveld G. Th.*, ed. undated.

Writings by Rietveld

1919
"Aanteekening bij Kinderstoel," in *De Stijl*, no. 9.

1926
"Niet een landhuis maar een gewoon huis," in *Bouwkundig Weekblad*, no. 44.

1927
De Stijl, nos. 79-84.
"Nut, constructie: Schoonheid, Kunst," in *i 10*, no. 3.

1928
"Inzicht," in *i 10*, nos. 17, 18.
"Kleine woningen te Utrecht," in *i 10*, nos. 17, 18.

1930
"Architectuur," in *De Werkende vrouw*, November-December.
"Beschouwing over het interieur," in *Het Bouwbedrijf*.
"De stoel," in *De Werkende vrouw*, no. 9.
"Interieur," in *Internationale leergang voor nieuwe architectuur*, Delft.

1932
"Landhuis te Breda," in *De 8 en Opbouw*, no. 3.
"Meubels," in *De 8 en Opbouw*, no. 10.
"Nieuwe zakelijkheid in de Nederlandsche architectuur," vol. 7, reprinted in *De Vrije Bladen*, Amsterdam.
"Zelfs te Weenen zit men nog niet bij de pakken neer," in *De 8 en Opbouw*, III.

1933
"Antwoord van Rietveld," in *De 8 en Opbouw*, no. 24.
"De nieuwe zakelijkheid in de architectuur: een lezing van architect Rietveld," in *Leeuwarder Courant*, February.

1934
"Bij het overlijden van Berlage," in *De 8 en Opbouw*, no. 18.

1935
"Vakverrotting," in *Bouwkundig Weekblad*, no. 47.

1937
"Indrukken op de Parijsche tentoonstelling,'' in *De 8 en Opbouw*, no. 18.
"Over de vorm van het meubel," in *De 8 en Opbouw*, no. 21.
"Rietveld schreef bij dit nummer," in *De 8 en Opbouw*, no. 20.

1938
"Kantteekeningen," in *De 8 en Opbouw*, no. 11.

1939
"De meubels van Oud," in *De 8 en Opbouw*, no. 2.
"Eenige uitspraken over architectuur gezien als een der plastische Kunsten," in *De 8 en Opbouw*, no. 6.

1940
"Aangifte," in *Bond van Nederlandsche Architecten*, Amsterdam.
"Woonhuis te Doorn 'Hoogzand'," in *De 8 en Opbouw*, no. 15.
[With Penaat W.] "Woonhuisje te Tongeren," in *De 8 en Opbouw*, vol. II.
"Zomerhuis te Petten," in *De 8 en Opbouw*, no. 15.

1941
"Een nieuwe platteground voor een volkswoning," in *Bouwkundig Weekblad*, no. 27.
"Een nieuwe volkswoning," in *De 8 en Opbouw*, no. 9.
"Het nationaal luchtvaart-laboratorium: archs. van Tijen en Maaskant," in *De 8 en Opbouw*, no. 10.
"Verbouwing Mij. voor Hypothecair Crediet," in *De 8 en Opbouw*, vol. 12.
"Verbouwing van den Schouwburg," in *De 8 en Opbouw*, no. 5.

1942
"Antwoord op de vraag: wat hoopt en verwacht U van de Nederlandsche architectuur in de Komende tijd," in *De 8 en Opbouw*, nos. 7, 8.

1946
"Industriële vormgeving," in *Open Oog*, no. 1.
Over Kennis en Kunst, lezing-cyclus over stedebouw, Amsterdam.

1947
"De verhouding tusschen beeldhouwer en architect," in *Nieuwe Utrechtsch Dagblad*, February.

1948
"Het interieur," in *Bouwkundig Weekblad*, no. 25.
"Oprichting van de N.I.V.A.G.," in *Bouwkundig Weekblad*, no. 26.

1949
"Aspecten van het nieuwe bouwen," in *Forum*, nos. 2, 3.
"Verleden en heden," in *Bouw*.

1950
"De bedoeling van de tentoonstelling," in *Schoonheid in huis en hof*, Amersfoort.
"Geen uitstalling, maar een overzicht," in *De Beyaard*, no. 7.
[With Vriend, J. J.] "Inrichting van woning en gebouw," E.N.S.I.E., vol. 9.

1951
"Die Nachkriegsarchitektur in Holland," in *Werk*, no. 11.
"Over architect Oud," in *Forum*, nos. 5, 6.
Rondgang. Cat. Tentoonstelling: Kunst & Kitsch, Gemeentemuseum, The Hague, October-November.
"Vacantiehuisjes," in *Goed Wonen*, no. 7.
"Een brief van Rietveld," in *Goed Wonen*, no. 4.

1953
[With Bep Eskes-Rietveld] "Kleur ontstaat waar de duisternis overheerst en het licht zich in wanhoop blijft verzetten," in *Goed Wonen*, no. 4.

1954
"De consequenties van het structuurplan van Utrecht voor de binnenstad," in *Bouwkundig Weekblad*, nos. 23, 24.
"In memoriam architect P. J. Klaarhamer," in *Bouwkundig Weekblad*, nos. 13, 14.

1955
"Mondrian en het nieuwe bouwen," in *Bouwkundig Weekblad*, no. 11.
"Moord op Utrechts binnenstad: of levensvoorwaarde voor een stad," in *Elseviers Weekblad*, October.
"Willem Penaat," in *Goed Wonen*, no. 11.

1956
"De Jaarbeursgebouwen in 40 jaren," in *Forum*, no. 3.
"Stands en hun inrichting vroeger en nu," in *Koninklijke Nederlandsche Jaarbeurs*.

1957
"Levenshouding als achtergrond van nijn werk," lecture at the Stedelijk Museum, Amsterdam.
"Ontwerper en materiaal," in *Visie*, no. 5.

1958
Forum, nos. 8, 9.

1961
Werk, November.

1963
Rietveld, 1924, Schröder Huis, Amsterdam [private ed.].

Photographic Credits

The relief drawings in the notes were made by Morena Casadio, Fabio Rodriguez, Antonino della Gatta, Lizzi Müller, and Ufficio Tecnico Cassina.
The prototypes presented in plates 7, 9, 12, 15, 18, 19, 20, 21, 23, 24, 34, 36, are part of the Stedelijk Museum collection, Amsterdam; those in plates 2, 3, 4, 8, 10, 17, 25, 27, 31, 32, 33, belong to the Cassina collection Meda; the one of plate 6 belongs to Gerard van de Groenekan; those in plates 1, 5, were made by Luigi Macalli, Milan; those in plates 11, 13, 14, 16, 26, 28, 29, 30, were made by Domenico Remondi, Albino (Bergamo); the one of plate 35 was made by Gennaro Capuano, Torre Annunziata (Naples).
The photographs for plates 7, 9, 12, 15, 18, 19, 20, 21, 23, 24, 34, 36, were made by the photographic studio of the Stedelijk Museum, Amsterdam; those for plates 1, 2, 3, 4, 5, 8, 10, 11, 13, 14, 16, 17, 25, 26, 27, 28, 29, 30, 31, 32, 33, were made by Giorgio and Valerio Lari, Turin; the photo for plate 35 was made by Enzo Marino, Naples.
Part of the background material was supplied by the Design Department of the Stedelijk Museum, Amsterdam.
The photographs on pages 8, 40, 57, 96, 103, 109, were taken by Gastone Dalle Vacche.